The Five Beasts of St. Hildegard

The Five Beasts of St. Hildegard

Prophetic Symbols of Modern Society

Reid J Turner

ISBN-13: 978-1505205312

ISBN-10: 150520531X

Dedicated to:

Richard, Brigitte, and Gabriel

Acknowledgments

All quotations from St. Hildegard are taken from *Hildegard of Bingen: Scivias*, translated by Columba Hart and Jane Bishop. The Abbey of Regina Laudis: Benedictine Congregation Regina Laudis of the Strict Observance, Inc. Paulist Press, 1990. Used with permission from the publisher.

All images are from a photographic reproduction of a copy of the original Rupertsberg manuscript (1165-1179) from A. Fuhrkotter, A. Carlvaris, eds. *Hildegardis Bingensis Scivias III, Corpus Christianorum Continuato Midiaevalis,* series 43A. 1978. Used with permission from Brepols Publishers.

Contents

Introduction 1

I. *Cane Igneo,* The Fiery Dog 7

II. *Leo Fulvone,* The Yellow Lion 17

III. *Equis Pallido,* The Pale Horse 27

IV. *Porco Negro,* The Black Pig 39

V. *Lupus Griseus,* The Grey Wolf 53

VI. The Antichrist 69

Conclusion 79

Appendix: The Beasts and Rev. 17 83

Notes 95

The Five Beasts of St. Hildegard

Introduction

Forty years ago, very few people, aside from a few Latin scholars in Germany, would have heard of St. Hildegard of Bingen (1098-1179), the twelfth century abbess who was recently named a Doctor of the Church. The rediscovery of her life and writings began when an American professor studying the Latin texts of Hildegard wondered why this prolific medieval mystic had never been translated into English:

> When I began working on the writings of Hildegard von Bingen in the late 1960s, I was the only one in this country doing so at the time, but I realized very quickly that there were lifetimes of research for hundreds of scholars in this and other English-speaking countries. Since most of her writings are very long and in complex Latin, readily available English translations were a necessary first step.[1]

Once the translations of her works began to appear in the 1980s, beginning with Hozeski's translation of her first book, *Scivias* (a shortened form of the Latin phrase, *Scito vias Domini,* "know the ways of God"), his enthusiastic prediction of Hildegard's popularity in the English-speaking world was soon realized. Today, most of her works have been translated and there is now an extensive bibliography of resources in English. It seems remarkable that eight-hundred years after her death, Hildegard would be heralded once again by the Church.

Prophetic visions about the future were only a fraction of Hildegard's works, but nevertheless have received a great deal of

1

attention due to their unusual imagery resembling the apocalyptic literature found in the Bible. But a vision is not exactly what Hildegard experienced with these revelations. Something much more dramatic and complex was happening to her than a visual experience or locution. In a letter written in 1175 to a monk named Guibert of Gembloux she described these experiences in terms of a light that comes to her:

> The light that I see is not local or confined. It is far brighter than a lucent cloud through which the sun shines. And I can discern neither its height nor its length nor its breadth. This light I have named 'the shadow of the Living Light,' and just as the sun and moon and stars are reflected in water, so are writings, words, virtues, and deeds of men reflected back to me from it. ...Whatever I see or learn in this vision I retain for a long period of time and store it away in my memory. And my seeing, hearing, and knowing are simultaneous, so that I learn and know at the same instant.[2]

One of Hildegard's more unusual example of these experiences was found in *Scivias*: Part III, Vision 11, a vision of five animals representing a succession of five historical eras she refers to as "ferocious epochs of temporal rule". Each era exhibits unique characteristics that reflect specific evils meant to inflict damage on the Roman Catholic Church. She refers to these beasts as the "forerunners" of the Antichrist, whose appearance immediately follows the fifth era. She states that they appear facing the west, signifying the approach of the end of the world. As the day closes with the setting of the sun, she tells us, so will the world be approaching its end at the time of the five beasts. Vision eleven begins with the beasts:

> *"Then I looked to the North and behold! Five beasts stood there. One was like a dog, fiery but not burning; another was like a yellow lion; another was like a pale horse; another like a black*

2

pig; and the last like a grey wolf."

Hildegard explains that each beast represents not just one, but a plurality of contending kingdoms as well as a specific period of time:

> **"These are the five ferocious epochs of temporal rule, brought about by the desires of the flesh from which the taint of sin is never absent."**

We will see that the symbolism of each beast points to a specific occasion of sinfulness. Hildegard first describes what she experienced in her vision and then breaks it down line by line, providing explanations of the individual symbol's meaning.

There are two additional and important sets of symbols corresponding to each beast meant to reflect the sins of these eras: five hills and five ropes:

> **"And in the West, before those beasts, a hill with five peaks appeared; and from the mouth of each beast one rope stretched to one of the peaks of the hill. All the ropes were black except the one that came from the wolf, which was partly black and partly white."**

Hildegard explains that *"...in these peaks is symbolized the power of carnal desire."* The ropes going from the mouth of the animal to the top of the mountain show that this power *"...will extend through the period in question."* She is revealing that the inclination toward a particular sin associated with the corresponding era will be evident from the beginning of the historical period to its end. The black color of the ropes reflects the persistence of people's attachment to that particular carnal sin, or, as she explains, *"...how far people are willing to go in their stubborn pleasures."*

The rope that comes from the mouth of the Grey Wolf, the last of the beasts, however, is both black and white. Hildegard explains that the part that is black represents those *"who put forth many evils"*, but the white part shows that *"...some will come from that direction who are white with justice."* It is these, she adds, who will *"...hasten to resist the son of perdition by ardent wonders."* The final of the five eras immediately precedes the time of the Antichrist and unlike the previous eras, will herald a time of great spiritual renewal in the Church.

She also states that these epochs will be brief, explaining that *"...these fleeting times will vanish with the setting sun."* It is the specific sequence of these relatively short historical eras that will form the key to recognizing that this prophetic vision is in the process of being fulfilled at the present time. The historical periods corresponding to the beasts and their specific evil must occur in a specific order. It's one thing to make a prediction of a single future event, but to predict a series of future events that follow each other is another matter. The fulfillment of a single prophecy validates its truth, but in the latter case a partial fulfillment of perhaps two or three of a series of five would legitimize the whole. In other words, if the first of two prophecies has been fulfilled, then one can anticipate the realization of the second. If two of three are fulfilled, the confidence in the third would even be higher, etc.

If multiple and well-defined eras can be recognized from recent history and if they are clearly characterized by the specific social evil symbolized by the corresponding beast, as well as occur in the correct order, then the fulfillment of Hildegard's vision may be unfolding today. And if our analysis is correct, we are currently in the middle or latter half of the era of the fourth beast and we can have a high degree of confidence that the events foretold to occur in the era of the fifth beast will transpire as described.

These visions were recorded in her first of many books, *Scivias*, which included visions that span the entire history of salvation, from Adam and Eve to the final judgment. The visions first caught the attention of the Archbishop of Mainz and then Pope Eugenius III. The Pope had the first part of the book (it took ten years to write) reviewed by his own commission, who

4

found her description of the visions and accompanying commentary free of doctrinal error.

To compare this vision to modern times it is necessary to perform three fundamental tasks. The first is to analyze recent history and identify a succession of historical periods that are brief and clearly distinguishable from one another. The second is to describe the characteristics and themes that are unique to each of the historical periods, looking for the emergence of a singular form of evil that affects not just broader Western society but the Catholic Church in particular. The third is to compare those themes with Hildegard's explanation of the respective symbol's meaning to see whether they correlate.

Hildegard would go on to write many more books, covering a variety of subjects including nutrition and medicine. She also wrote sacred music, plays, and poetry (she was the most prolific composer of chant in the twelfth century). She also left us with hundreds of pieces of her personal correspondence, much of it with kings, queens, and popes. Pope Eugenius had intended to declare her writings inspired but this was cut short by his death.

The process of Hildegard's formal canonization, which began shortly after her death, was never completed which demonstrates that her legacy was quickly fading from the Church's memory. Eight centuries later, in 2012, not only was her canonization fully realized, but the plan by Pope Eugenius to elevate her writings was finally accomplished when Pope Benedict XVI formally named her a Doctor of the Church, a title that she now shares with St. Thomas Aquinas, et al.

When the symbolic elements of Hildegard's vision are understood the way she intended them to be, then interpreting the vision is neither difficult or requiring much in the way of guesswork. Her explanations of the symbolism are not vague or overly complex. A basic knowledge of recent history and a recognition of the unique spiritual crises that the Church has had to endure in the last century and a half will lead one to suspect the modern world was the object of her visionary experience.

Hildegard's world was essentially Europe, living at the time when Christendom would soon reach its zenith. The Roman Catholic religion in the Europe of recent history has been disappearing, undergoing a process sadly referred to as dechristianization. Her vision reveals this in a remarkable way, but also offers hope to us in the present time that this will soon change, but not without a period of turbulence.

I

Cane Igneo, The Fiery Dog

"One is like a dog, fiery but not burning; for that era will produce people with a biting temperament, who seem fiery in their own estimation, but do not burn with the justice of God."

The Historical Period: 1870-1914

In our attempt to apply these visions to the twentieth century a valid historical period must first be identified. We can use the year 1900 as a starting point, since, like any year, it must belong to some particular historical era. On a broad scale, most historians would refer to 1900 as belonging to what is commonly called the Age of Imperialism, of which the year 1900 is generally considered its zenith. It would be difficult to find another time in European history when as many monarchs were internationally recognized as emperors.

Yet it was also the age of European liberalism, a form of unregulated capitalism that saw great wealth created as a result of industrialization. Imperialism and liberalism had merged into something altogether new. These were not like the Roman Empire, whose military adventurism accumulated vassal states. Motivated by profit, the empires that were flourishing in 1900 colonized their possessions for the purpose of economic expansion. The Western empires needed natural resources and new markets for their mass-produced goods.

While periodization of history is normally a difficult task, the year this era ended is unusually easy to determine. Historians naturally have different opinions on the importance of certain events and will divide history somewhat subjectively. The late historian Eric Hobsbawm suggested that specific dates or years are often chosen for convenience in trying to identify a distinct period. Yet he discovered a remarkable exception to this:

> History is not like a bus line in which the vehicle changes all its passengers and crew whenever it gets to the point marking its terminus. Nevertheless, if there are dates that are more than convenient for purposes of periodization, August 1914 is one of them.[1]

He adds that August 1914 was "...one of the most undeniable natural breaks in History."[2] Whatever year one chooses to mark as the beginning of the age to which the year 1900 belongs, historians are in universal agreement that it ended with World War One.

The era is also sometimes referred to as the "Age of the Monarchs". Before the outbreak of the war Europe had 30 reigning monarchs, but by the war's conclusion there were only three left. Within a few years of the war's start, Emperor Franz Joseph of Austria, who described himself as "the last monarch of the old style," would be dead after a sixty-seven year reign.[3] Czar Nicholas II of Russia and his family would be murdered by Bolshevik assassins while posing for a photograph, and Wilhelm II of Germany would flee into exile. In a sudden and brutal way, by the end of WWI the age of the Monarchs was finally over, an era that began on December 25, AD 800 with the crowning of Charlemagne as Emperor of Europe.

Most of the monarchs abdicated, as it was also an age of expanding democracy and contracting royal power. The nineteenth century saw most of Europe progressing towards the democratic ideals of the Franco-American revolution.

8

Hobsbawm noted that "...after 1870 it became increasingly clear that the democratization of the politics of states was quite inevitable. The masses would march on to the stage of politics whether the rulers liked it or not"[4] After the war, however, they would turn around and march back, as totalitarianism would come to dominate the European stage.

What were the circumstances of the Roman Catholic Church in 1900? Up to a point, the preceding century was not unkind to the Church. In France, much of the property lost in the French revolution was restored, as was the monarchy. In Britain, parliament passed the Roman Catholic Relief Act of 1829 which led to the re-establishment of dioceses and their long-awaited re-connection to Rome. In America, where Catholics had been generally unwelcome from the time of the revolution, the doors swung open and their population would surge due to to German, Irish and Italian immigration.

But the Church's fortunes sharply reversed in the 1870s. The Church lost the Papal States in 1870 and found itself not only without a sovereign home, but the subject of an hostile Italian nationalist rule. Also in 1870 the Franco-Prussian War broke out which would change the map and power structure of Europe. It also affected the mood of Europeans toward Catholics. The rapid and decisive victory of the primarily Protestant Prussian forces over the humiliated French was viewed by many as a victory over the Catholic Church. Immediately following the war, Germany, under chancellor Bismarck, instituted the *Kulturkampf,* a series of laws that were discriminatory against Roman Catholics. Failure of compliance with the laws led to the imprisonment of almost two thousand priests. Other European nations followed suit. In his 1873 encyclical, *Etsi Multa,* Pope Pius IX likened the situation to a war:

> Some of you may perchance wonder that the war against the Catholic Church extends so widely. Indeed each of you knows well the nature, zeal, and intention of sects, whether called Masonic or some other name.

When he compares them with the nature, purpose, and amplitude of the conflict waged nearly everywhere against the Church, he cannot doubt but that the present calamity must be attributed to their deceits and machinations for the most part. For from these the synagogue of Satan is formed which draws up its forces, advances its standards, and joins battle against the Church of Christ.[5]

In France, the secularists proceeded to extract the Church from French society. Education was their top priority, increasing the education budget from 46 million francs in the late 1870s to 300 million by the outbreak of WWI.[6] In 1886 a law was passed which totally secularized elementary education, bringing about what historian Michael Burleigh called "...the end of a venerable tradition based on the unity of religion, knowledge, and moral instruction."[7] he noted that throughout Europe, all forms of Christianity were under siege:

> The 19th Century commenced with the near universality of the confessional state under which one religion, one Christian denomination, was privileged by the state, while other denominations and religions were tolerated at best. By the century's close, these arrangements had been abandoned, or modified, almost beyond recognition.[8]

After the Bourbon Restoration in France (1814), the Revolution was generally viewed by the French as a low point in their history. Yet in the 1880s, the secular French government took a different view of Robespierre, et al., and decided the brutal treatment of the king and the clergy was worthy of a celebration. July 14 was made a national holiday and the revolutionary "Marseillaise", up to then a prohibited song, was adopted as the national anthem. According to Burleigh this was primarily motivated by anti-clericalism, "...with the storming of the Bastille being reinterpreted as deliverance from the stranglehold of superstition."[9]

In Spain, the Carlists were defeated in the Third Carlist War (1872-1876). Carlism was a Spanish movement born from a legitimacy dispute over the succession to the throne of King Ferdinand in the 1830s. The Carlist ideology was rooted in traditional Catholicism and they remained opposed to secularization and the ideals of the French Revolution which were gaining support among the upper classes as well as the court. Their defeat meant a victory for secularization and resulted in the seizing of ecclesiastical property and new discriminatory laws. The loss of the Papal states initiated a turning of the tide for the Church and is clearly enough of a historical break to mark the beginning of an era that was historically unique to the rest of the century and the era that followed, particularly with respect the Catholic Church.

Symbolism of the Fiery Dog

If we begin with the assumption that 1870-1914 represents Hildegard's era of the Fiery Dog, we can now examine it to judge how well this era exhibits the symbolic meaning of the beast. A Fiery Dog is not exactly what she saw in the vision. She describes the color of the dog as "fiery", but a fire that does not burn:

"...for that era will produce people with a biting temperament, who seem fiery in their own estimation, but do not burn with the justice of God."

Here we have the description of a temperamental people whose passion is misdirected or perhaps purely evil; they only seem fiery to themselves. The meaning of this symbolism applies to the people of the era and their unique cultural or social behaviors that would reflect an attachment to a particular sin.

One possibility that comes to mind is that these are references to the numerous enemies of the Church that this era produced. There was no shortage of tirades aimed at Christianity during the era from people like Nietzsche, who would declare the Christian God dead, or Marx, who claimed that religion was

11

the "opiate of the people", or Freud, who called religion a "crutch". Certainly, among most of the intellectuals of the period belief in religion had faded or even turned into open hostility. While it must be admitted, however, that this is something that is not unique to this era, nevertheless some of these enemies of religion would prove to be profoundly destructive to the world even to this day.

The symbolism, however, suggests something more specific than a varied group of intellectuals that are hostile toward religion in general. If we focus our attention on Hildegard's use of the word "justice", we can gain a better idea of what she had envisioned. The reason the dog is not on fire is because it references people who "...*do not burn with the justice of God,*" suggesting that being on fire as a symbol of intense passion for something is not necessarily a bad thing, but only if it is a passion for God's justice. "Justice" is being used here in its role as the chief cardinal virtue, the "moral quality or habit which perfects the will and inclines it to render to each and to all what belongs to them."[10] A perfect example is paying fair wages, which is why the failure to pay a man his due wages constitutes one of the four "sins that cry to heaven" (CCC 1867).

Social Justice at the Turn of the Century

In this sense the end of the 19th century was indeed a time when there was a general lack of justice. The wealthy ate well, traveled, and enjoyed the creative cultural life in the European cities. The art of the Impressionists, depicting pleasant scenes of afternoons in an outdoor bar or along a river, leads one to envision the *Belle Epoch* as an era of general prosperity. It was a relatively peaceful era and industrialization had produced affluence for some. It was also an era of optimism; scientific discoveries and inventions during this period would change the world forever.

But there was a dark side as well, a side that was immoral and corrupt. The good times were for the wealthy few and did not extend to everyone, not to the scores of men, women, and children working in factories or farms who were being economically mistreated. One historian describes the darker side of the period:

> There were big buildings, big factories, big battleships, big fortunes. There were also anxieties, frustration and political and social disorders. The brilliance of Western civilization, for many, was only the glitter of the fake and the heartless. The rising new aristocracy of industry and politics no longer opposed the old nobility but had come to terms with it. The snobbery of wealth reinforced the snobbery of birth and both classes gained materially and both became spiritually bankrupt. There was irresponsibility on the part of the rich and powerful that resulted in a host of subtle and not-so-subtle ethical and moral evasions.[11]

This spiritual bankruptcy and irresponsibility did not go unnoticed by the Church. It was on May 15, 1891 that Pope Leo XIII issued one of the great encyclicals in papal history, *Rerum Novarum*. It became the definitive statement of the Church's position on issues pertaining to social and economic justice. In the introductory paragraph Leo explains exactly what was wrong in that era:

> The elements of the conflict now raging are unmistakable, in the vast expansion of industrial pursuits and the marvelous discoveries of science; in the changed relations between masters and workmen; in the enormous fortunes of some few individuals, and the utter poverty of the masses; in the increased self-reliance and closer mutual combination of the working classes; as also, finally, in the prevailing moral degeneracy. The momentous gravity of the state of things now obtaining fills every mind with painful apprehension; wise men are discussing it; practical

men are proposing schemes; popular meetings, legislatures, and rulers of nations are all busied with it -- **actually there is no question which has taken a deeper hold on the public mind**.[12] [Emphasis mine]

The words "justice" or "injustice" occur twenty-two times in the brief encyclical and represent the foundation for the arguments based on natural law for private-property rights, fair wages, and the right to form unions. The main focus of the encyclical is on the working poor and the responsibilities of employers in treating them fairly. Leo charged that "...a small number of very rich men have been able to lay upon the teeming masses of the laboring poor a yoke little better than that of slavery itself."[13] He further complained, "...it has come to pass that working men have been surrendered, isolated and helpless, to the hardheartedness of employers and the greed of unchecked competition."[14]

The Rise of Socialism

To a growing number socialism was the answer. Leo recognized that the working classes were drawn to its promise of equality for all. Socialism was on the rise; shortly before the publication of *Rerum Novarum* the Second International was formed in Paris, a federation of more than three-hundred socialist parties and trade unions representing twenty countries. Leo above all wanted to make it noticeably clear in the encyclical that socialism was not an answer, condemning communism as "unjust":

...Their contentions are so clearly powerless to end the controversy that were they carried into effect the working man himself would be among the first to suffer. They are, moreover, emphatically unjust, for they would rob the lawful possessor, distort the functions of the State, and create utter confusion in the community.[15]

14

Like Hildegard's Fiery Dog, the socialists indeed had passion for justice for the working poor, but that passion resembled mob justice, not the justice of God.

While the art of the Impressionists rarely reflected the darker side of the era, it was on full display in the literature of the period. One can read about the struggles of the various social classes in the novels of Emile Zola in France and Thomas Hardy in England, among many others. They expose the rigid moralistic and hypocritical religiosity of the bourgeois society, and its unjust treatment of the labor class. This is not the same world of the classic European bourgeois, a social caste with rights and privileges that had lasted in Europe for centuries. With the progress of the industrial revolution, the old bourgeois, with money and standing, naturally stepped into the role of liberal capitalist.

Pope Leo's encyclical was critical of both the wealthy capitalists as well as the socialists, to him both lacked the "justice of God", a concern to which he remained focused his entire papacy. Pius XI would later acknowledge the work of his predecessor in his own 1937 encyclical condemning communism, *Divini Redemptoris*. The origin of socialism's appeal was the misery experienced during the previous era,

> If we would explain the blind acceptance of Communism by so many thousands of workmen, we must remember that the way had been already prepared for it by the religious and moral destitution in which wage-earners had been left by liberal economics.[16]

But it was the Marxists who openly advocated violent revolt that Pope Leo feared the most. Their vision of the state, he affirmed, would "...act against natural justice, and destroy the structure of the home," leading to a "...leveling down of all to a like condition of misery and degradation".[17] It was not Leo's first official condemnation of socialism; in 1878, in his encyclical

Quod Apostolici Muneris, he called the teachings of socialism "depraved", and a "...deadly plague that is creeping into the very fibers of human society and leading it on to the verge of destruction."[18]

Summary

Hildegard's vision describes a people with a "biting" temperament, "snapping", and "fiery" (passionate) but only in their own minds because "they do not burn with the justice of God." By focusing on the word justice, the symbolism is a fitting description of the followers of Marx and the ideology that would dominate and menace much of Europe for decades and remains a danger to this day. The unjust bourgeois, rentier, and aristocratic classes, on the other hand, would be swept away in the Great War. The communist threat was growing and consolidating its strategy for reshaping the world, a world where the concept of God's justice would be replaced by man's concept of justice. As demonstrated by Papal fears of its growing influence, it proved to be the dominant threat to the Church in Europe during the era of the Fiery Dog.

II

Leo Fulvone, The Yellow Lion

"Another is like a yellow lion; for this era will endure martial people, who instigate many wars but do not think of the righteousness of God in them; for those kingdoms will begin to weaken and tire, as the yellow color shows."

The Historical Period: 1914-1945

In 1922 Thomas Mann lamented,

There is at hand the ending of an epoch: the bourgeois, humanistic, liberal epoch, which was born at the renaissance and came to power with the French Revolution.

It may have outwardly appeared to him that the epoch was coming to an end, but in reality, by 1922 it was a distant memory. By that time Communist Russia had already established labor camps for political opponents, Mussolini had become prime Minister of Italy, Hungary was being run by the military, and the NAZI party was founded in Germany.

Between 1918 and 1922 Mann's Germany was an exceptionally dangerous place to have political aspirations as nearly 400 political assassinations took place. One would have expected that in the wake of the horrors of WWI, a war-weary Europe would have sought peace and reconciliation, not militarism. But war sentiment persisted and intensified.

Out of the ashes of the Great War quickly emerged a very different Europe with regard to both its map and its people. 1914 was the major turning point. Hobsbawm, and others, connect the two wars, referring to the period as the "Age of Catastrophe," also calling it the "Age of Total War".[1] It began with the biggest and most destructive war ever fought and ended with one that was exponentially worse.

It is clear, even at first glance, that Hildegard's description of the meaning of the symbolic yellow lion bears a disturbing resemblance to this "Age of Total War". She called the people of this era "martial people," or perhaps better translated as "war-mongering", people that would produce many unjust wars. In comparing Hildegard's description of the symbolism to the era, images of swastikas, jackboots, and Communist May Day parades fit right in. If there was ever a period of time in modern Western history that was dominated by mentality of war it was 1914-1945. Historians have struggled to grasp the reasons for this.

Nationalism

Historically, Germany is generally considered a very Christian country, Lutherans in the north and Catholics in the south. On the other hand, The German people of this era, suggests Burleigh, may not have been as religious as is commonly assumed:

> Outsiders, who are routinely deaf to the nuances of religion in Germany, are often perplexed as to how Nazism could have taken root in a Christian nation, without over-troubling themselves with the question whether one part of that proposition is true.[2]

How else could one explain the popularity of the National Socialists. Hitler may have believed in some type of god, but it was not the Christian one: "I shall never come to terms with the Christian lie ...our epoch will certainly see the end of the disease of Christianity."[3] As Prime Minister of Italy, Mussolini's brand

18

of nationalism was also hostile to Christianity declaring, "...the Fascist conception of the state is all-embracing; outside of it no human or spiritual values may exist, much less have any value."[4]

Part of what influenced the social mentality of the people of this era was the outcome of the Paris Peace Conference in 1919, where the fate of the now defeated central powers would be decided. Dismantling the Ottoman, Austrian and German empires turned out to be no easy task. Borders had to be re-established for the former subject states and in some cases new states were created that never existed. Since nationalist movements had been organized and supported during the previous age by one of the empires in order to undermine a competing empire, common ethnicities (nations) were to be the logical priority in drawing borders.

Yet this turned out to be impractical; ethnic commonality did not always include language or religion, and what nation, wherever its borders are placed, would not have at least some minority presence? In the end, the "nation", as a concept of a union based on a shared nationality became the "nation-state", a Western idea of ethnic plurality coexisting with a dominant nationality. The victors of the war decided that minority groups would exist within the newly formed nation's borders and their rights of citizenship would be guaranteed by the state. Drawing the specific borders was made easier by this innovation, with the process even having become somewhat arbitrary.

While minority rights treaties were imposed on the new governments to guarantee the safety of these groups, there was no international entity with the ability to enforce them. The genocide of Turkey's Armenian community from 1915-1918, which left over a million dead, should have been an early warning sign that creating nation-states out of the dissolved empires was destined to render minorities unprotected.

Yet it was viewed by the nationalists themselves as hypocritical for countries like the U.S.A. and the British Empire to impose such treaties on others when they did not respect the rights of their own minorities; civil rights laws in the U.S. would not be enacted until the 1960s. Neither were the British very sensitive to the rights many of their imperial subjects, particularly the non-white ones. Historian Mark Manzower points out the credulity of this kind of thinking, "...the underlying premise of this thoroughgoing liberalism was that assimilation into the civilized life of the nation was possible and desireable".[5] He explains that WWI,

> ...accelerated the Turkification of the Ottoman Empire. The attempt to murder the Armenians, ...was the logical extension of the nationalist program in Istanbul. ...Many in the West were filled with horror; few bore in mind that it was the introduction of the western conception of the nation-state into the multi-national societies of the Near East that had led to massacre in the first place.[6]

The unworkable combination of the opposing concepts of nationalism and the state led to the genocides, a word invented in the 1940s to describe the abhorrent phenomenon particular to this era.

In his celebrated book, *Humanity: A Moral History of the Twentieth Century,* ethicist Jonathan Glover theorizes that the warmongering was the result of a strong sense of national honor, radicalized by the popular ideology known as social Darwinism. He writes, "Behind social Darwinism was the idea that nation-states were the units of evolutionary selection. There was an idea of the 'nation' almost as a person and central to this was national honour."[7] People suddenly became enthusiastic for war:

> In August 1914 most of the belligerent countries were swept with enthusiasm. In Berlin, when mobilization was announced, the crowd sang the hymn 'Now thank we all our God.' In Britain too there was a wave of patriotism. [Lord] Kitchener had

hoped for 100,000 volunteers in the first six months, and for 500,000 in all. There were 500,000 in the first month and nearly 2,000,000 in the first six months.[8]

Burleigh was mystified as to the reason for this:

> Like the Italian fascists and Japanese militarists, the German National Socialists regarded war as a release from what they called the 'lingering disease of peace,' a particularly pathological view of the condition that most human beings aspire to.[9]

In London, crowds would gather and cheer the march to war until late in the night. Bertrand Russell recalled these days in his autobiography: "During this and the following days I discovered to my amazement that average men and women were delighted at the prospect of war."[10] It should be remembered that the First World War was the meaningless result of unnecessary military alliances. It was triggered by the assassination of the Archduke of Austria by a Serbian student with ties to a nationalist movement. He was arrested and tried by Serbian authorities who never wanted war with Austria. The death toll was at least six million lives, with some estimates far higher.

Moving into the 1930s, historians describe the dark and militaristic mood of the times:

> The newsreels show endless waves of marching, uniformed men and wildly gesticulating orators haranguing cheering crowds of people. The emotions and hatreds unleashed by the first World War had not been arrested and together with new grievances and animosities created a dark wave of revolution that ultimately was to engulf the continent.[11]

By the mid-1930s eighteen countries covering two-thirds of Europe were totalitarian, predominantly military dictatorships ruling by the exercise of terror. One historian cynically referred to totalitarianism as "...the single significant contribution of the first half of the twentieth century to Western political thought."[12] In terms of the combination of intolerance of opposition, control of press and education, and endowing themselves with unlimited power, Fascism and Communism were virtually identical.

Catholic historian Paul Johnson sees this time as the triumph of moral relativism:

> Relativism took many different forms but all put the real or imagined needs of 'society' (in practice the group in power) before the claims of an absolute code of right and wrong. ...Hitler and the Nazis called the criterion of morality 'the Higher Law of the Party' and followed it to launch world war and kill nearly six million Jews. Lenin and Stalin called it the 'Revolutionary Conscience', and its dictates led to the murder or death in the Gulag of 20 million 'enemies of the people.'[13]

George Orwell read *Mein Kampf* in 1940 and saw in Hitler's vision, "...a horrible, brainless empire in which, essentially, nothing ever happens except the training of young men for war and the endless breeding of fresh cannon-fodder."[14] Hitler's appeal, according to Orwell, was based on his understanding that people wanted more than just a life of comfort. Hitler gave their lives meaning, people, "...at least intermittently, want struggle and self-sacrifice, not to mention drums, flags, and loyalty-parades."[15] Four years later Orwell noted the consequences of this on the mentality of the average European:

> In the chaos in which we are living, even the prudential reasons for common decency are being forgotten. Politics, internal and international, are probably no more immoral than they have always been. But what is new is the growing acquiescence of the public opinion in the face of the most atrocious crimes and sufferings, and the black-out memory

which allows blood-stained murderers to turn into public benefactors overnight.[16]

The Yellow Lion

An interesting aspect of the illumination of the lion which accompanies the text of the manuscript is that it is not painted yellow but colored in a reddish shade. Differences between the textual description of the symbol and its corresponding illumination are common throughout this particular manuscript of *Scivias* (Rupertsberg) which was produced in Hildegard's abbey's own scriptorum and under her immediate supervision. It demonstrates that they were either the work of Hildegard herself or drawn by someone she personally directed. In later manuscripts produced after her death differences between the text description of the beasts and the corresponding illuminations do not appear.

The confusion is resolved in the written text. Hildegard makes it clear that the lion does not start out yellow, but turns yellow as the era approaches its end, reflecting a progressive weakness, "...for those kingdoms will begin to weaken and tire, as the yellow color shows." Hildegard would not have had a problem painting the Yellow Lion red, whereas the illuminator of a later manuscript would not have considered it. We come across another example of this in the next era, the Pale Horse.

The fall of Nazi Germany was as much internal as external. After the power of the Third Reich had reached its apex in 1942, the tide turned and the military began to implode. The lion was weakening due to its own lack of any moral compass. The yellow spinelessness of the Nazis in defeat was on display at the Nuremberg trials as the common defense by the murderers of Jews and others in the camps was that they were under obligation to obey orders, with the audacity of thinking this would protect them from the noose.

Another pathetic attempt at self-vindication on display at the trials was to offer no defense at all. When Field Marshall von

23

Runstedt was questioned in Nuremburg, asked if he ever considered assassinating Hitler, he responded that he was not a traitor. German historian Joachim Fest maintained that this mentality was common at the trials, referring to it as a "pseudo-morality". "[A] soldier can betray his country, his people, his honor, and his responsibility for the lives of his subordinates, but not a man to whom he has sworn an oath." The historian explains that this is just an example of cowardice:

> It is not difficult, then, to discern behind this defence, which employed pseudo-morality to stylize into an attitude of selfless devotion to duty what was really only a lack of moral fiber, the distinctive mark of a weak opportunism which characterized the overwhelming majority of the top-ranking German officers of the period.

This was the downfall of Germany. When Hitler refused to accept that he was losing, all the while planning new offensives and refusing to order retreats, the weak officers blindly went along.

Another sign of Germany's cowardice towards the end was the drafting of boys belonging to the Hitler Youth Organization (Hitlerjugend). Aged 12-18, they were called up along with old men to form Germany's last line of defense. They were massacred by the Russians during the Battle of Berlin yet continuing to fight even after Hitler's suicide.

Summary

Hildegard's vision of the lion described an era of people that embraced the powerful fascist militarism, overflowing with malice, and cowardly following it to its own self destruction. Surely the thirty-one years between 1914-1945 exhibited these characteristics to the extreme, a display of humanity at its worst.

There were indeed brave and decent people who risked their lives protecting the Jews and others targeted by the Nazis. Glover acknowledges the role of religion in this. "...[O]ften the values which led people to take risks to help came from religious commitment."[17] At the conclusion to his history of the twentieth century, Glover, not a friend of religion, nevertheless makes the admission: "Those of us who do not believe in a religious moral law should still be troubled by its fading."[18] The eras that follow will attest to the gravity of that warning.

III

Equis Pallido, The Pale Horse

"Another is like a pale horse; for those times will produce people who drown themselves in sin, and in their licentious and swift moving pleasures neglect all virtuous activities. And then these kingdoms will lose their ruddy strength and grow pale with the fear of ruin, and their hearts will be broken."

The Historical Period: 1945-1991

The famous series of pictures taken during the final stage of WWII showing FDR, Winston Churchill, and Joseph Stalin sitting together at the Yalta Conference in February of 1944 are full of smiles. Perhaps they reflected the relief that victory in Europe was assured even though the fighting continued. But they might have also been just for the cameras. The cost of war to the British would be a half million lives and would leave the country broke, with much of London destroyed. Sadly, Churchill had spent his whole adult life overseeing the disintegration of the greatest Empire the world had ever seen.

But for Americans the war in the Pacific continued and the pictures revealed that Roosevelt's health was further deteriorating. Stalin entered the war late but lost the most, over twelve million soldiers and another ten million civilians. Stalin, a man with little concern for human life, anticipated the spoils of victory; his smile was probably the most genuine. The three would be responsible for the post-war reconstruction of Europe, the Soviets in the east, the British and Americans in the west. That Stalin might prove to be a greater threat to Europe than Hitler was not given due consideration by Roosevelt, who needed his help fighting the Japanese.

Soon after the war's end, President Harry Truman began to object to Stalin's interference in the politics of countries in Eastern Europe. Historians universally regard the period that follows as the "Cold War" era, a period which began at some point between 1945-50 and lasted until the collapse of the Soviet Union in 1991. It was in this era that communism reached its apex, both geographically and in its capacity to destroy human life. Russia had returned to her imperial past, encompassing more than half of Europe and threatening the rest.

Conversely, under the protection and financial support of the United States, Western Europe experienced almost steady economic growth from the implementation of the Marshall Plan in 1948 to the end of the era. West Germany was to become one of the biggest economies in the world. For numerous historians, the story of the cold war era is the story of a particularly brutal form of socialism and its battle with the West by way of espionage and proxy wars, but for much of Western Europe it was the experience of an economic miracle. While American influence on the cultural life of Europe during the first two of Hildegard's eras was limited, its power and influence would be felt during this one.

The Cultural Revolution

Looking at this era from the Church's perspective, however, the geopolitical conflicts were secondary. Hildegard explains that the people of these times will *"...drown themselves in sin, and in their licentious and swift-moving pleasures neglect all virtuous activities."* The key word here is "licentious"; Hildegard was describing a period of progressive moral decay and dissolute behavior. From a traditional Catholic perspective, it would be difficult to find a historical period in modern history where a common understanding of sexual morality underwent such dramatic change than what occurred during the Cold War era, particularly the 1960s and 1970s. Hobsbawm was not the only historian to sub-divide the era, referring to these decades as "The Cultural Revolution," a time of social upheaval in the West that included revolutionary changes in attitudes regarding human sexuality.[1]

The starting point for this may have come at the very outset of the era. In 1948 the first of the two Kinsey Reports was published, *Sexual Behavior in the Human Male,* which would be followed by *Sexual Behavior in the Human Female* in 1953. Bestsellers and translated into numerous languages, these books were influential in inaugurating the sexual revolution. They were the first of their kind to openly discuss sexual practices that Western society traditionally considered taboo. Kinsey relied on surveys and interviews. Curiously, the validity of the data Kinsey used in the books has been regarded by many as questionable, and the methods used for obtaining the information ethically and legally suspicious.

The revolution occurred on both sides of the Atlantic. British author Peter Hitchens points to the changing legal perspective on literature in Britain resulting from the numerous obscenity trials in the 1950s-60s as a contributing factor to the sexual revolution in his country:

> This outcome had been achieved by the route of arguing 'literary merit' to justify the breaking of old taboos. It is a curious country which abandons an entire moral code on the grounds that immoral works might be an uplifting read, but that is roughly what we have done. Literary merit is so utterly subjective that there will always be some professor or parson willing to bestow a good

reputation on the vilest garbage.[2]

Hitchens discusses American influences over various parts of British society that occurred after the war, sexual morality being among the most profound:

> American attitudes towards divorce and adultery, the collapse of American puritanism ...under the blows of Kinsey and the contraceptive pill, fanned out across this country like an infectious disease. ...The triumph of Elvis Presley, whose influence was rightly seen as revolutionary by American Conservatives, brought an entirely new thing into our lives -- the sexualization of the young combined with the narcotic emotional power of rock music. ...Presley dug beneath the fortifications of British sexual reserve, leaving them so weakened that John Lennon and Mick Jagger could knock them down completely.[3]

The most important event in the history of the sexual revolution was undoubtedly the legal approval of the birth-control pill for public use. It received FDA approval in 1960 in the U.S. and was legalized a year later in the U.K. and Germany. The social significance of this was profound; it liberated women from having to attend to birth control before considering whether to engage in sexual encounters. This new freedom had the broader sociological effect of changing the perception of sexual relations as a means for procreation to primarily a means of experiencing pleasure. Within a couple years of the pill's approval, millions of women were using it.

Hildegard also explained that the people of this era would pursue "swift moving pleasures" and "neglect all virtuous activities." Virtue is the opposite of sin and she was probably not referring to specific virtuous acts but the opposing conditions of dissolute behavior versus temperance and self-control. Hildegard wrote often about the antithetical nature of specific sins with their corresponding virtue. In her second book of visions *Liber Vitae Meritorum, The Book of the Rewards of Life*, she specifically lists and describes thirty-five sins and their antithetical virtue.

This lack of temperance was increasingly evident in culture as a whole, particularly in fashion, dance, literature, etc., but perhaps most powerfully in cinema. By the late 1960s the strict Hays Code, that had enforced a list of prohibitions on what could not be shown or said in American films, was routinely being ignored. This was due to the pressure of European competition which had little such oversight and took full advantage of the new artistic license. In 1968 the code was finally abandoned and replaced by a formal rating system, freeing up Hollywood to make films with few restrictions on content.

One film star that personified the new conception of sexual morality in the early 1960s was the French actress Brigitte Bardot. Author Theodore Zeldin, in his classic *The French*, sees her as more than just a reflection of changing social customs:

> The significance of Brigitte Bardot is not that she aroused male lust, but that she represented an attempt by a generation to find a new style of relationship in which sex and sexuality had a more central role.

In 1968 the birth control pill was approved in France and by then Pope Paul VI recognized that it was time for the Church to react to the rapidly devolving notions of morality. He responded with a long-awaited encyclical that would settle the matter of artificial birth control. Paul begins *Humanae Vitae* by confronting Western society's progressive moral decay:

> Everything therefore in the modern means of social communication which arouses men's baser

passions and encourages low moral standards, as well as every obscenity in the written word and every form of indecency on the stage and screen, should be condemned publicly and unanimously by all those who have at heart the advance of civilization and the safeguarding of the outstanding values of the human spirit. It is quite absurd to defend this kind of depravity in the name of art or culture or by pleading the liberty which may be allowed in this field by the public authorities.[5]

While the essential purpose of the encyclical was to clarify and re-affirm the Church's prohibition on the use of artificial birth control, the foundation of his argument was the nature of the family and the meaning and purpose of conjugal acts. It was a condemnation of the sexual revolution and a major disappointment for many, including churchmen.

While the encyclical was well received outside Europe and North America, it was essentially rejected in the West by both secular governments and organizations like the United Nations. Opposition from within the Church was widespread; from the hierarchy to the laity petitions were circulated and calls for the encyclical's repudiation. Most bishops did not want to go to their respective diocese and expressly forbid the use of artificial birth control; and many did not. This led to the development of a means to circumvent Church teaching.

What resulted was a new and dangerous theological concept; the appeal to one's personal conscience as a guide in matters of sexuality and contraception. The Church would be viewed by an increasing number of Catholics as no longer the sole authority on matters of sexual morality. This theological misconception of the role of the conscience would spread to other teachings of the Church which the laity found inconvenient or too controversial. Pope John Paul II would condemn this error in the encyclical *Veritatis Splendor* in 1993

(This will be discussed in detail in the following chapter).

Symbolism of the Pale Horse

As with the previous animal symbols Hildegard was given the understanding that the symbolism of the horse represented the people produced by the era and the particular sin to which they are attached. This is also signified by the rope in the mouth of the horse with which the animal fastens itself to the mountain. The mountain is the expression of a particular sin, in this case licentiousness, and the rope indicates that such behavior would span the length of the era. The blackness of the rope reflects the preponderance of the sin in Western society and its success in inflicting damage on the Church.

Like the Yellow Lion, the Pale Horse is not painted pale in the accompanying illumination. It is depicted in rather robust health and colored in a greenish tone. In a comment on the vision some years later Hildegard further noted that the horse was unbridled, symbolizing a wild nature and a lack of control. Hence, the paleness of the horse should be viewed as a symbol of the natural consequence of the lack of restraint, a progressive illness or weakening. She explains that the society would experience a change as the era proceeded:

> *"...these kingdoms will lose their ruddy strength and grow pale with the fear of ruin, and their hearts will be broken."*

Since the reference to *"these kingdoms"* should be understood in a sociological sense, the "ruddy strength" would correspond to the licentious behavior of the people during the era. Hildegard saw a vision of a healthy but wild horse gradually turning pale as though from a disease.

From a Catholic perspective it was a spiritual disease. The symptoms of this malady and the damage this was causing to Western society were everywhere to be found. The Cold War era saw divorce rates double in America and Europe, cohabitation became commonplace, and homosexuality would go from generally regarded as a psychological pathology whose practice was illegal to achieving broad social acceptance and legal protections. Other symptoms of this social disease would include the decline in birth rates below the replacement level in numerous Western countries, suicide rates (which increased dramatically in the 1970s-80s), and abortion rates (which exploded in the 1970s), etc. The West was literally killing itself off.

It was not just social diseases that plagued the era, but physical ones as well. The immune-system disease which came to be known as AIDS was discovered in 1981 and had been spreading among an ignorant public for possibly as long as a dozen years. There was no cure or effective treatment and it led to certain death. It was also discovered to be in the nation's blood supply. The disease would eventually kill over 600,000 Americans.

Neither was the Church immune to the consequences of this cultural revolution. Even though the revelations of a pattern of sexual abuse of children by Catholic priests were not uncovered until the mid-1990s, the abuse itself, and the cover-ups, primarily occurred during the Cold War era, peaking in the 1970s-80s. In his 2010 annual Christmas address to the Roman Curia, Pope Benedict XVI reacted bitterly to a new rash of accusations regarding abuse of minors in Europe by laying the blame on the culture of the 1970s:

> In the 1970s, pedophilia was theorized as something fully in conformity with man and even with children. ...It was maintained – even within the realm of Catholic theology – that there is no such thing as evil in itself or good in itself. There is only a "better than" and a "worse than". Nothing is good or bad in itself. Everything depends on the circumstances and on the end in

view. Anything can be good or also bad, depending upon purposes and circumstances. Morality is replaced by a calculus of consequences, and in the process it ceases to exist.[6]

Official reports on the abuse commissioned by the various bishops' conferences have understated the extent of the violations. The numbers they reported could only include credible public accusations of abuse. Yet how many victims had chosen not to make them, sparing themselves and their families from the stress and humiliation of revealing something horrific that was hidden in their past? How many have died before they even had a chance to make an accusation? The true extent of the abuse could be double or triple the reported numbers.

Probably the best critique of the social and moral corruption of this era at the time came by way of a commencement address by Russian Nobel laureate Alexander Solzhenitsyn to what must have been a disheartened Harvard graduating class of 1978. The school had just awarded him an honorary doctorate. Since Solzhenitsyn had been exiled to the West after years in the gulag, one would expect a lecture on the appreciation of freedom, but the problem he had with the West was its abuse of freedom:

> ...Destructive and irresponsible freedom has been granted boundless space. Society has turned out to have scarce defense against the abyss of human decadence, for example against the misuse of liberty for moral violence against young people, such as motion pictures full of pornography, crime, and horror. This is all considered to be part of freedom and to be counterbalanced, in theory, by the young people's right not to look and not to accept. Life organized legalistically has thus shown its inability to defend itself against the corrosion of evil.[7]

By the word "legalistically" Solzhenitsyn was referring to a society organized solely on the letter of the law, a law however that had no absolutes to serve as its foundation. Like the previous eras, the West was abandoning absolutes for a new set of laws that were relativistic, in this case to ensure freedom for everyone. It is as if a choice, whatever it is, should be considered good as long as it is made freely.

Solzhenitsyn asked:

> ...Is it true that man is above everything? Is there no Superior Spirit above him? Is it right that man's life and society's activities should be ruled by material expansion above all? Is it permissible to promote such expansion to the detriment of our integral spiritual life?[8]

The Harvard speech also spoke of general weakening in Western society:

> There are telltale symptoms by which history gives warning to a threatened or perishing society. Such are, for instance, a decline of the arts or a lack of great statesmen. Indeed, sometimes the warnings are quite explicit and concrete. The center of your democracy and of your culture is left without electric power for a few hours only, and all of a sudden crowds of American citizens start looting and creating havoc. The smooth surface film must be very thin, then, the social system quite unstable and unhealthy. ...[The] fight for our planet, physical and spiritual, a fight of cosmic proportions, is not a vague matter of the future; it has already started. The forces of Evil have begun their decisive offensive. You can feel their pressure, yet your screens and publications are full of prescribed smiles and raised glasses.[9]

Summary

The social history of the period of time corresponding to the Cold War was striking in its remolding of attitudes on sexuality and the family. The West eventually found itself in serious moral decay but refused to acknowledge or address the obvious contamination it was causing Western society. It was truly an era uniquely characterized by licentious behavior and neglect of virtue. By the 1980s, those at the vanguard of the cultural revolution were now teachers, bankers, lawyers, etc. using materialism and pleasure-seeking to distract their attention from the damage they had a hand in creating. Hildegard's horse had turned deathly pale.

IV

Porco Negro, The Black Pig

"Another is like a black pig; for this epoch will have leaders who blacken themselves in misery and wallow in the mud of impurity. They will infringe the divine law by fornication and other like evils, and will plot to diverge from the holiness of God's commands."

The Historical Period: 1991-Present

We have now arrived at the era within which we are currently living. It began in 1991 with the collapse of the Soviet Union and the end of the Cold War. Since it is a historical period that is still unfolding, we will not have the same benefit of the numerous studies and commentaries by historians that aided us in our analysis of the previous eras. On the other hand, the era is now over twenty years old, and since we are presently experiencing it, it should be possible to assess the characteristics of the period that future historians may use to describe it. As symbolized by the rope that goes from the mouth of the beast to the top of the mountain, the evil that marks this period will be present throughout the era.

There were many changes after 1991 besides the end of communism and a redrawing of the map of Europe. Despite the promise of peace and stability it brought, America seized the opportunity to expand NATO alliances to former Soviet republics. Along with the bombing of Serbia, these moves were seen by Russia as an unwelcome intrusion into its former sphere of influence. A more cooperative relationship between the two superpowers, rendering NATO alliances unnecessary, seemed of no interest to policymakers, and the antagonism between the U.S. and Moscow has unsurprisingly since been renewed. While the political systems in Western European countries remained the same, coalition governments managing welfare states, one major difference with the previous era was the establishment of the European Union (EU) in 1993, and later, in 2002, the European Monetary Union.

The EU does not represent full political integration, though the framers pushed hard for it. The people of Europe refused to surrender their individual nation's sovereignty, leaving it more of a partnership with the purpose of enjoying numerous benefits derived from open borders and common laws benefiting trade and commerce. However, the European Monetary Union did not benefit every country equally and has been in and out of crisis since 2008. The European Union's future is questionable.

International economic cooperation was an undoubted theme of the era and future historians might refer to it as the "Age of Globalization". On the other hand, should the EU break up, or international trade agreements fall apart, it would be the failure of globalization and its consequences that might end up characterizing the era or mark its end. Others might call it the "Age of Consumerism" as debt financing to fuel consumption and maintain or improve standards of living became the norm. An economy's over-dependence on debt for growth is clearly unsustainable. Also, the progress of telecommunications and how it had changed the world will surely be central to understanding this era. Yet the connection of these themes to the symbolism of the Black Pig and the description of its meaning is not readily apparent.

It is similar to the era of the Fiery Dog, where we uncovered multiple themes to which different historians attributed various levels of importance. But recall that a single theme stood out from the perspective of the Church. Analyzing the present era from the Church's frame of reference and her recent reactions to the times, and with an understanding that Hildegard's visions are referring to spiritual crises, we arrive at a similar end.

The Catholic Perspective

At the beginning of this era John Paul II made some interesting observations in his 1993 encyclical *Veritatis Splendor*, which primarily addressed a specific moral crisis that emerged in the Church as a result of the backlash following the publication of the encyclical *Humanae Vitae*. He criticized an approach to matters of sexual ethics evident among many priests, bishops, and instructors in seminaries which emphasized the role of the "conscience" in making personal decisions regarding issues already settled by the magisterial teaching of the Church. He attacked the notion that moral decisions can be based on what he called an "individualist ethic".

Veritatis Splendor has been referred to as his most important encyclical because he redirects his argument against the role of conscience to address the broader moral crisis in the Western world. In the aftermath of the collapse of communism in Europe he warned of an equal danger to the West, the danger of freedom when it becomes divorced from natural law. He saw a connection between moral relativism and totalitarianism that was irrespective of specific political ideologies:

> Today, when many countries have seen the fall of ideologies which bound politics to a totalitarian conception of the world — Marxism being the foremost of these — there is no less grave a danger that the fundamental rights of the human

person will be denied and that the religious yearnings which arise in the heart of every human being will be absorbed once again into politics. This is *the risk of an alliance between democracy and ethical relativism,* which would remove any sure moral reference point from political and social life, and on a deeper level make the acknowledgment of truth impossible. Indeed, 'if there is no ultimate truth to guide and direct political activity, then ideas and convictions can easily be manipulated for reasons of power. As history demonstrates, a democracy without values easily turns into open or thinly disguised totalitarianism.[1]

While he was addressing an internal Church question with the encyclical, he nevertheless recognized a danger facing Western society, that without moral absolutes, "...ideas and convictions can easily be manipulated for reasons of power." Democracy would be no panacea and relativism could transform it into a form of totalitarianism which would attack the Church and society from a legal perspective. This would be a new offensive on a different front to inflict damage on Christ's Church; and one manifestation of this would be attacks against the Church's teaching on the family.

John Paul probably was aware that his warning to the West was too late. Deeply concerned about an increasing number of laws being instituted in the West that affected the family, John Paul II declared 1994 the "Year of the Family". In his attendant *Letter To Families,* he condemns laws permitting abortion:

> ...How can one morally accept laws that permit the killing of a human being not yet born, but already alive in the mother's womb? The right to life becomes an exclusive prerogative of adults who even manipulate legislatures in order to carry out their own plans and pursue their own interests.[2]

A year later John Paul II produced the encyclical *Evangelium Vitae,* where he took aim at the laws that were being established in various countries that continued to devalue human life:

> At the same time a new cultural climate is developing and taking hold, which gives crimes against life a new and - if possible - even more sinister character, giving rise to further grave concern: broad sectors of public opinion justify certain crimes against life in the name of the rights of individual freedom, and on this basis they claim not only exemption from punishment but even authorization by the State, so that these things can be done with total freedom and indeed with the free assistance of health-care systems. ...The fact that legislation in many countries, perhaps even departing from basic principles of their Constitutions, has determined not to punish these practices against life, and even to make them altogether legal, is both a disturbing symptom and a significant cause of grave moral decline."[3]

He was referring to laws advancing euthanasia, abortion, and assisted suicide. Those of an "even more sinister character" included the possibility of manipulating human life to harvest organs.

The Pope recognized that there was a noticeable shift in the type and nature of many of the policies being signed into law by Western governments. He considered advances in technology coupled with declining moral standards and radical individualism as responsible. He held the leaders of those governments responsible:

> I urgently appeal once more to all political leaders not to pass laws which, by disregarding the dignity of the person, undermine the very fabric of society.[4]

But the generation of leaders since the 1990s have not been, in general, the same type of people as their predecessors. They were, and are, almost all pro-abortion, pro-feminist, and hostile toward Church teaching on a variety of moral issues. How could they have turned out so different from the leaders of the past?

Political Correctness

It was around the early 1990s, that conservatives in America, primarily politicians, took aim at an alarming trend affecting educational institutions. They described it as "political correctness" (PC), a phrase borrowed from the Soviets for whom it referred to one's loyalty to the party lines. It was adopted and used in a pejorative sense to describe a phenomenon that had been infiltrating university campuses for decades but had remained relatively unchallenged. But it was beginning to influence other parts of society. Sociologist Paul Hollender defined the phenomenon as it related to education:

> PC is, above all, a climate of opinion, a complex of social and institutional pressures and threats, beliefs and taboos which have come to dominate the campuses and academic public discourse over the past quarter century. ...There are at least five areas to which PC applies and where it succeeded in imposing a fair amount of conformity. They are 1) race-minority relations; 2) sexual and gender relations; 3) homosexuality; 4) American society as a whole; 5) Western culture and values. In regard to each, PC prescribes publicly acceptable opinions and attitudes. ...Deviation from the norms of PC may result in public abuse, formal or informal sanctions, administrative reproach, delayed promotion, difficulty finding a job ...etc.[5]

It took some time before PC was recognized and confronted in the public arena. The revelation of the phenomenon was likely generated by the popularity of the book, *The Closing of the American Mind,* by University of Chicago professor Allan Bloom. His conclusion was that once what we now call political correctness came to dominate the educational institutions, true academic inquiry became impossible. The two are incomparable since the former represents the rejection of rational intellectual thought.[6] This is the same formula we saw in John Paul II's *Veritatis Splendor,* that by removing or changing moral reference points, (which is what underlies political correctness), the consequence makes "...the acknowledgment of truth impossible." While Bloom's book ignited criticism of PC and hopes of its demise, it had no effect on its dominance in the universities.

America was not the only Western country where this was taking place. In *The Abolition of Britain,* Peter Hitchens called it the "new conformism" and "...the most intolerant system of thought to dominate the British Isles since the reformation."[7] To Hitchens, it was at least as destructive in Britain as it was in America:

> In the thirty years before the 1997 election, a long and profound set of changes in the British way of life had just brought to maturity a generation to whom the past was not just a foreign country, but a place of mystery that was easier to mock than to understand. ...Into the vacuum left by the end of British self-confidence a new conformism had come rushing, probably more powerful than the one which went before. This is often dismissed, half-jokingly, with the casual phrase 'political correctness'. But this imported expression does not even begin to encompass the power and danger of the thing.[8]

The result of political correctness is that certain issues are no longer subject to debate since debates are supposed to be rational processes. It is easier to accuse those who disagree of chauvinism, intolerance, or worst of all, of being a racist. At this point we can ask what we might expect from the generation of students who were subjected to this form of brainwashing as they moved into their chosen professions or whatever role they would later play in society. This is not hard to do; one simply needs to recollect the social developments of recent decades.

Think of the names of those in positions of leadership from the early 1990s on: presidents, prime ministers, parliamentarians, congressmen, judges, etc.; most of them were sitting in a university classroom sometime in the late 1960s or later. Their support of same-sex marriage or civil union laws, gender ideology, abortion, etc., in some cases contrary to the will of the people they govern, is just a natural manifestation of the consequence of their generation having submitted to political correctness. It is all natural to them.

Social Engineering

In 2009, British historian Paul Johnson asked the same question that we are asking here: "What are the salient evils of our time?" At the top of his list was social engineering, which he described as " ...the idea that human beings can be changed, improved and moved about as though they are quantities of cement or concrete."[9] Johnson observed that "...today, virtually all regimes, whether democratic, dodgy, or outright totalitarian, practice social engineering."[10] He further argues that the foundation of social engineering is the triumph of moral relativism, which he made the central theme of his own history of the twentieth century, *Modern Times*. Again, it is the same formula John Paul II warned Western democracy to avoid. The purpose of social engineering, Johnson points out, is that it is "...designed to engineer the population in a direction designated by government."[11]

Social engineering, of course, has been tried many times. In the case of the Nazis, it promoted the concept of a master race and was used to justify genocide. In communism it forced commitment to the party ideology and justified repression. It is not hard to make the case that here in the West social engineering by governments is pervasive, but what is interesting is the question of what the engineering is attempting to force people to think or do. Unsurprisingly, the engineering that has emerged in the present era is all about the very same issues the sociologist Hollander listed as the goals of political correctness: race-minority relations, sexual and gender relations, homosexuality, American society, and western culture and values.

Social engineering in the West is what political correctness handed it when it graduated from educational institutions and invaded governmental institutions beginning in the 1990s. Regarding the question of what would happen to the generation of students who were first subjected to political correctness as they moved into their respective roles in society; they became the social engineers of today.

As serious a danger as social engineering is for Western society in general, it is particularly menacing to the Roman Catholic Church. In a homily given in 2010, the soon to be Cardinal Raymond Burke, lamenting America's abandonment of its Judeo-Christian heritage, described the state of the country as reaching the very state of totalitarianism of which John Paul II warned:

> More and more we witness the violation of the most fundamental of norms of divine natural law in the policies and laws of our nation. ...The law more and more dares to force those with the sacred trust of caring for the health of their brothers to violate the most sacred tenets of their consciences, ...a society which pretends to take the place of God in making its laws and giving its judgments, ...a society in which those in power decide what is right and just, according to their desires and convenience.[12]

The first line of Cardinal Burke's quote reflects the gravity of what is happening; the various objectives of the social engineers are violations of divine natural law. Promotion of same-sex marriage or civil unions would have been politically suicidal only a few decades ago; today, one's opposition to such concepts will come with a social or political price to pay.

Symbolism of the Black Pig

Hildegard's description of the symbolism of the Black Pig is unique in that it focus' only on the leaders of the era:

"...for this epoch will have leaders who blacken themselves in misery and wallow in the mud of impurity. They will infringe the divine law by fornication and other like evils, and will plot to diverge from the holiness of God's commands."

The language is suggestive of a culture that, led by corrupt and immoral leaders, has descended into something resembling Sodom and Gomorrah. The previous era, the Pale Horse, was focused on the licentiousness and lack of temperance of the times, and accurately described the cultural revolution that peaked in the 60s and 70s. In time the energetic horse became sick and began to turn pale as the social consequences of the behavior emerged. The present era, however, seems to have started the party back up, and many from that generation has grown up to become our national and local leaders who actively support and promote acts that, as Hildegard's foretells, "infringe the divine law."

To describe an individual or group as pigs who "wallow in the mud of impurity" is very strong language. While there is no shortage of scandals, sexual and otherwise, involving politicians, not all the leaders of today are corrupt, perverted, or adulterers. On the other hand, it is interesting to note that behavior which at one time would have ruined a politician's career is routinely ignored by the public. A recent article discussing the phenomenon by journalist David Lightman listed the many scandal-ridden politicians whose careers have survived the scandal:

> If there's a line of demarcation when shame lost its status as a poison dart for a political career, it came in the late 1990s. President Bill Clinton's dalliance with Monica Lewinsky was graphically described day after day. Clinton was impeached but not removed from office, and he left the presidency in 2001 with stellar approval numbers. He now is more personally popular than any other living former president. ...At the same time, behavior once regarded as deviant or suspicious became commonplace. Divorce, let alone sexual affairs, were no longer career-killers. Neither was admission of drug use. Reports of such actions lost their ability to shock.[13]

This era's leader's personal lives may not be the only way they "wallow in the mud of impurity". Hildegard's also states that they will also "plot to diverge from the holiness of God's commands." This description applies to many if not most of the leaders of the West. The Latin word that is translated with the verb "to plot", can also be translated, "to scheme, devise, or conspire." Some examples are the passing of laws and policies that redefine the nature of the family to include homosexual relationships, laws that encourage the killing of unborn children and promoting the practice around the world, legalization of euthanasia, etc. Such as these have been and will continue to be forced on society whether it wants them or not. The original goals of political correctness are now in their forced implementation phase.

Also, many of today's leaders exhibit a tendency toward hypocrisy. Consider the behavior of politicians who claim to be practicing Catholics, yet tirelessly campaign for the promotion and availability of abortion, birth control, and homosexual marriage. Tony Blair was received into the Church in 2007 despite his open support for these condemned practices. He later regretted approving the law in 2005 legalizing civil unions for homosexuals, but only because it did not go far enough and include marriage. In the early 1990s the Clintons fought for the protection of traditional marriage. President Clinton had signed into law the Defense of Marriage Act, which he later regretted, conveniently reversing his position on homosexual marriage along with Mrs. Clinton in time for an election campaign.

Over a million people filled the Avenue des Champs-Elysees in Paris to support traditional marriage in 2013. President Francois Hollande completely ignored them and signed homosexual marriage into law shortly after the demonstration. Yet personally, Hollande always preferred cohabitation to marriage, having separated from his partner with whom he had four children. His most recent partner walked out on him when a magazine reported that he was having an affair behind her back with an actress. Hollande is another fine example of Hildegard's fourth beast. On the other side of the channel, when the Queen of England, who is also the head of the Church of England, gave royal assent to homosexual marriage, it was clear that the era of the Black Pig was in full swing. This may be exactly what Hildegard meant by leaders who "wallow in the mud of impurity".

In 2007 Britain passed the "Equality Act", which prevents businesses from discriminating against homosexuals. What is noteworthy is that there were no exemptions allowed for religious reasons, and many Christians have since suffered as a result. A harsh reaction to the legislation came from Cardinal Cormac Murphy-O'Connor who saw where this would lead:

My fear is that, under the guise of legislating for what is said to be tolerance, we are legislating for intolerance. Once this begins, it is hard to see where it ends... What looks like liberality is in reality a radical exclusion of religion from the public sphere.[14]

Surprisingly, Cardinal O'Connor was the bishop that received Blair into the Church. The leaders of today have no hesitation in enacting laws that are not only incompatible with divine law, but legally force Christians to act contrary to their religious beliefs, a de facto repeal of freedom of religion. What can this be leading to? It should be disquieting; the era is not yet over.

What might mark the end of the era of the Black Pig and the beginning of the Grey Wolf? If we compare what marked the change in the previous historical eras, we will be anticipating a shift in the geopolitical power structure of the world. The structure since 1991, in the wake of the collapse of the Soviet Union, has been that of American hegemony, both militarily and economically. There is much at stake if the U.S. abdicates or is forced out of this critical role. The focus should be on America, and a significant decline of her dominant position in the world will likely mark the beginning of the end of the present historical period.

Summary

We asked earlier what would happen to the generation that grew up under the pressures of political correctness when they eventually took their places in society as adults. Many of those who found themselves in positions of power became today's social engineers, matching the description of the leaders in Hildegard's vision, institutionalizing the PC agenda as politicians, judges, philanthropists, etc. That agenda is symbolized as "mud of impurity" that "infringes the divine law". The damage to the Church has been severe, evidenced by declining mass attendance and vocations, scandals, defiance of Church teaching, etc., accelerating the dechristianization of the West.

We can also ask what would happen to the next generation, those who would come of age in the present era, as they become the leaders in the future. Western society has changed dramatically since the previous era. From the symbolism of the ropes, we know that the social engineers of today have been and will continue to be successful in their aims. The next generation of leaders will likely take social engineering to its logical next step, crushing the last of the opposition to their agenda with a greater effort, perhaps one that includes violence and imprisonment.

Political correctness in the universities has increased in intensity since the 1990s; this is evident by comparing the many campus rules, curriculum, and faculty today with those of the 1970s and 1980s which now appear mild. There is a reason for this that is worth noting. In the 1960s college attendance soared in the U.S. which was the result of three trends. One was that the post WWII baby boom generation had begun turning eighteen in 1964. Another was that a college degree was increasingly perceived as desirable and necessary for personal advancement. The third was the G.I. Bill, which included education benefits for combat veterans from WWII; in 1966 it was expanded to include peacetime soldiers. Universities and colleges were desperate for instructors.

As a result, and because of tenure, most of the professors teaching through the 70s, 80s, and into the 90s had begun their careers in the 60s. In the mid-nineties, a dramatic shift took place in higher education as they began retiring *en masse*. They were replaced by those who had a vastly different type of education from the instructors they succeeded, creating an ideological shift to a more radical embracing of the goals of PC. This was anticipated; graduate students at the beginning of the 1990s understood their degrees would soon lead to a position. The generation of leaders today will seem mild by comparison to those of tomorrow

V

Lupus Griseus, The Grey Wolf

"And the last is like a grey wolf; for those times will have people who plunder each other, robbing the powerful and the fortunate; and in these conflicts they will show themselves to be neither black nor white, but grey in their cunning. And they will divide and conquer the rulers of those realms: and then the time will come when many will be ensnared, and the error of errors will rise from Hell to Heaven."

The Final Beast

Recognizing the era of the Grey Wolf should not be difficult; Hildegard's descriptions of what will take place during this period are more detailed than the previous eras. Once the epoch commences and the events began being manifested in society, the vision can be a guide for what to expect in the years ahead. What will be found alarming, however, is the violent nature of the period. Hildegard describes the era as a period of intense social unrest leading up to the appearance of the Antichrist, the "error of errors".

While she is specific about what will take place during the era, knowing exactly how these things will transpire in advance is not possible. While speculation based on the direction of current events may be helpful and will be briefly explored here, there are numerous possible scenarios that could match Hildegard's explanation of her vision.

53

The Symbolism of the Ropes

We get an important piece of information about the era of the Grey Wolf from Hildegard's earlier comment concerning the ropes that stretch from the mouth of each beast to the mountain peak, representing the people's attachment to the particular evil and its continuance throughout the length of the era. She explains why the rope going from the mouth of the Grey Wolf is both black and white:

> *"All the ropes are black except the one that comes from the mouth of the wolf, which is partly black and partly white. ...though the one that symbolizes greed is partly black and puts forth many evils, yet some will come from that direction who are white with justice. And these latter will hasten to resist the son of perdition by ardent wonders."*

This reveals two important pieces of information about the era. The first is that the evil of the era is greed, which is unusual since Hildegard does not explicitly state the name of the specific sin that characterized the other four periods. Secondly, that during this period the Roman Catholic Church will experience a spiritual reform or renewal.

Unlike the other four periods, where the rope is black, symbolizing the people of the era's acquiescence to sin, this one will produce some people who are "white with justice". This renewal could take many forms but the fact that the generation that experiences this "...will hasten to resist the son of perdition" suggests that it is above all a spiritual rebirth, and a powerful one. But this will only be true of "some", implying a minority. Whether it is a large minority or a small one is not specified, evidence of moral and spiritual uprightness growing within the Church in a manner unseen in the previous will be evident early in the era.

After a century and a half of spiritual warfare the tide will have finally turned in favor of the Church, resulting in a strengthened faith among some that will enable them to preserve their faith as they endure the persecutions of the Antichrist. Further clarification of this period of renewed faith is revealed in the part of the vision that immediately follows the five beasts, Hildegard's vision of Christ and his Bride (discussed below).

"White with Justice"

What did Hildegard mean by the phrase "white with justice"? Like the unjust era of the Fiery Dog, this may be a reference to social justice. However, Hildegard makes it clear that in the time of the Grey Wolf those who consider themselves economically disenfranchised will take justice into their own hands. The phrase could also be a general reference to faithfulness emanating from the Church at the time, but Hildegard might have chosen better words to explain the symbolic meaning of the color if it was a popular spiritual revival that the Church would experience. With the help of her scribe, Volmar, she might have chosen words like righteous, faithful, godly, devout, etc.

In a more specific sense, it could be a reference to justice as the virtue that stands opposite to the unjust nature of the era and its violent uprisings motivated by greed. The juxtaposition of the black part of the rope, representing greed and unjust thievery, with the white part, symbolizing faith and justice, suggests the possibility of a clash between the two. The Church could even be the channel of God's justice. Those bent on destroying and plundering society will receive justice from God through his faithful ones, possibly but not necessarily, implying some type of confrontation, military or otherwise.

One can find numerous books consisting of various compilations of prophecies made by Catholics who claim to have the charism of prophecy. Hildegard's prophetic visions are always included; she is considered one of the greatest among them. Yet most of them exclude her vision of the five beasts. One reason for this may be that it does not share the two most common elements found in the prophecies pertaining to the time just before the Antichrist. Many Catholic prophecies from the past speak of a return to monarchy and the re-conquest of Europe by a "great king" followed by a "period of peace" of unspecified length.

By interpreting those who are "white with justice" as people who will confront and defeat the forces of unrest and revolution, which would consequently be followed by a period of peace, is not in contradiction with those elements common to so many other Catholic prophecies. While many of those prophecies state it explicitly, Hildegard's description of the era excludes those events but does not expressly preclude their possibility.

The concept of a Christian uprising motivated by love for God and a desire to protect his Church is not unprecedented in modern times. The Carlists of Spain militarily defended her traditional Catholic legacy against the forces of secularism for generations. They provided over a 100,000 of its soldiers to fight the communists during the Spanish civil war and were renowned for their heroism on the battlefield. Carlism has experienced a revival since General Franco's death in 1974. They were even seen at a counterdemonstration during the 1989 celebrations of the bicentennial of the French revolution. Spanish philosopher Rafael Gambra, a former Carlist soldier, exclaimed, "If God should need Carlism to save Spain once more, it will emerge from the shadows."[1]

Vision of Christ and the Bride

The question of the fate of the Church in the era of the Grey Wolf is clarified by analyzing the part of the vision that immediately follows the five beasts. These include symbolic images of Christ and that of His Bride (the Church).

56

Hildegard explains that certain parts of their respective physical body represent a chronological timeline of events leading up to the reign of the Antichrist. In the fascinating illumination accompanying the text, Christ is pictured sitting in the corner of a building, representing the cornerstone of the Church:

And lo, in the East I saw again that youth whom I had first seen on the corner of the wall of the building where the shining and stone parts came together, clad in a purple tunic. I now saw him on the same corner, but now I could see him from the waist down. And from the waist down to the place that denotes the male he glowed like the dawn.

She saw the same image of Christ, younger looking, in the previous vision (Bk. 3, Vis. 10). But in that vision the area below his navel was not visible. By the eleventh vision the time of the five "epochs of temporal rule" had begun, symbolizing the arrival of the last days, consequently, the rest of his body had become visible to Hildegard. The Church is

57

represented by the figure of a bride:

*And I saw again the figure of a woman whom
I had previously seen in front of the alter that
stands before the eyes of God, ...but now I saw
her from the waist down. And from her waist
to the place that denotes the female, she had
various scaly blemishes, and in that latter
place was a black and monstrous head.*

The Bride which had appeared in an earlier vision only
from the waist up, is also now seen fully complete. This
reflects, similar to the image of Christ, that the last days had
arrived. Importantly, Hildegard declares that by that time the
Church will be "...replete with the full number of her children"
(Chap. 13).

Along with the figure of Christ, the individual parts of

her body from the waist down represent a chronological series of events leading up to the destruction of the Antichrist. Between her waist (navel) and the "place that denotes the female," appear "various scaly blemishes." This corresponds to the time of the Grey Wolf in which violence and social unrest persist as well as persecution of the Church. But in this part of the vision the violence directed at the Church is distinct from the persecution by the Antichrist which Hildegard explains will come later:

> *...Before the time in which the son of perdition will try to perfect the trick he played on the first woman, the Church will be harshly reproached for many vices, fornication and murder and rapine. How? because those who should love her will violently persecute her* (Chapt. 13).

This also corresponds to the same place on the body of Christ, from the waist to the "place that denotes the male", which Hildegard reveals is when the Church will be made perfect prior to the appearance of the Antichrist. Notice the different perspectives on the same event. From the Church's point of view what will take place is a harsh reproach, but from Christ's perspective it is a "perfection in fortitude":

> *"For until the time of the son of perdition, who will pretend to be the man of strength, His* [Christ's] *faithful members will be perfected in fortitude and He will be splendid in the justice of his righteous worshippers"* (Chapt. 9).

Again, we have a reference to the word justice; it is the result of being "perfected in fortitude" by means of a "harsh reproach". Hildegard is giving us an explanation of the fate of the Church in the era of the Grey Wolf; it will have to experience a purification by enduring a period of oppression before it produces a generation that will be able to successfully confront the persecutions of the Antichrist.

It was suggested earlier that a confrontation between Europe's dwindling population of Catholics and growing number of Muslims was not inconceivable given the recent experience of Christians in the Middle East and North Africa. In this part of the vision Hildegard gives us another clue that points to who might be responsible for this persecution of the Church. She states that "those who should love her will violently persecute her." While *everyone* should love the Church, and that could be the meaning here, the statement is more likely alluding to a specific group.

In one sense atheists should love the Church, but in another sense one would not realistically expect them to. The same could be said for communists, radical feminists and homosexuals, occultists, etc., people who obstinately adhere to beliefs that the Church officially condemns. Muslims, on the other hand, pray five times a day, fast, and disapprove of homosexuality and abortion. They place a high value on the family and orthodox Muslim women are expected to guard their virginity until marriage. Muslims today have been born into a heretical offshoot of Christianity that affirms the historical person of Christ but denies his divine nature, yet they adhere to much of the same natural law as Christians are expected to. They should be joining the Church rather than persecuting her.

Another clue to who might be responsible for this persecution is the symbolic color of the wolf. Hildegard states that, "in these conflicts they [those responsible for the social unrest] will show themselves to be neither black nor white, but grey in their cunning," Unlike the rope, which is part black and part white, contrasting those who are purely evil and those who are "white with justice", this group of people are the result of the blending of the two colors. There is something very evil about them as well as something apparently good. This could refer to various social entities today but not to extent that it would to radical Muslims. The color white, reflecting their apparent high moral standards and claim to worship the same God as Christians, is blended with the color black, representing their extreme violent tendencies toward those they consider infidels, especially Christians.

One might be tempted to think that "those who should love her" could reference a group within the Church. But we need to consider that the nature of the persecution clearly involves physical violence. It would not seem likely that aggression would break out among members of the Church. Moreover, Hildegard refers to the persecution during this era as a "harsh reproach", a punishment meant to chastise the Church for its unfaithfulness. Those within the Church that have been disloyal to Church teaching are more likely to be the recipients of the chastisement.

"Fornication, Murder, and Rapine"

Hildegard tells us that the Church will have been declared guilty of these vices by the time of the era of the Grey Wolf, but she does not tell us in what manner the sins were committed. Since we are now approaching the era of the Grey Wolf, we would want to consider the question of whether the Church of today bears the guilt of these sins to the extent that it would invite the severe punishment from God described herein.

In the case of fornication, the first thing that comes to mind are the sex abuse scandals that have rocked the Church in recent decades. The question to ask is whether the Church of today has adequately responded to the crisis, both in a physical and spiritual way. It is beyond the scope of this study to make a judgment on that question, but new revelations of abuse and cover ups continue to appear in the news. Has the vocations process been changed? Have the seminaries been purged of instructors who teach a sexual morality that differs from Church magisterium? Have any books advocating such teachings been condemned? Where are the threats of excommunication? The Church has powerful tools to enforce her laws but elects not to employ them.

Then there is the issue of "conscience" discussed in previous chapters; it has replaced the Church as the authority for personal decisions on sexuality for many Catholics. This obviously has the support of many priests and ecclesiastical authorities in the West, causing scandal to many within the Church. On this basis alone one would have to answer the question of whether or not the present Church is guilty of fornication in the affirmative, at least to some extent.

Rapine is plunder and theft. Financial scandals within the Church have been well documented by a number of highly respected journalists. Pope Francis had pledged to clean up the finances of the Vatican, promising accountability and transparency. At the time of this update to the book (mid-2016), that effort apparently has been abandoned.

The Church of Hildegard's Germany continues to collect a "Church tax" *(kirchensteuer)*, and it has been reported that priests are expected to withhold certain sacraments from Catholics who refuse to pay it. Dioceses in America have paid out billions in settlements for abuse claims that left many of them filing for bankruptcy protections. While the settlements are justified and necessary, innocent parishioners have to bear much of the financial responsibility.

Of the three sins for which the Church today bears a measure of culpability the easiest to prove is murder. The Church could face the accusation for a number of reasons, like supporting an unjust war or the discovery of murderous intrigues at the higher levels of the Church hierarchy. The latter likely only occurs in fictional novels and the former is at present simply not conceivable.

The answer comes from the refusal of the vast majority of Church authorities to enforce the Church's prohibition on the use of birth control. Contraception itself is not murder, but according to the magisterial teaching of the Church it bears the same guilt. While the injunction against contraception has been formally established Church teaching since the twelfth century, it goes further back to St. Augustine. His argument centered on an interpretation of Genesis 38:8-10, the story of Onan, whom God had struck dead for engaging in *coitus interruptus* with his dead brother's wife:

> ...for intercourse, even with one's lawfully wedded spouse, can take place in an unlawful and shameful manner, whenever the conception of offspring is avoided. Onan, the son of Judah, did this very thing, and the Lord slew him on that account. Therefore, the procreation of children is itself the primary, natural, legitimate purpose of marriage. Whence it follows that those who marry because of their inability to remain continent ought not to so temper their vice that they preclude the good of marriage, which is the procreation of children (*De Conjugiis Adulterinis* 2, 12).

Another long-held canon is more direct:

> If someone to satisfy his lust or in deliberate hatred does something to a man or woman so that no children can be born on him or her or give them to drink so that he cannot impregnate or she cannot conceive, let this be treated as homicide. (Regino of Prum, 1840, 2. 89)

In the twelfth century these condemnations of contraception were incorporated in canon law and remained so until the twentieth century. The teaching was reaffirmed by Pope Pius XI in his encyclical on marriage, *Casti Connubii* (1930), and again in *Humanae Vitae*. (For a full treatment of this injunction, see John C. Ford S.J., Germain Grisez, Joseph Boyle, John Finnes, and William E. May, *The Teaching of Humanae Vitae: A Defense*, San Francisco: Ignatius Press, 1988).

While it is clear that the three vices have infiltrated the Church, whether they have reached the degree to deserve a chastisement can only be known when the "harsh reproach" becomes evident.

The Image of the Antichrist

The time of the Antichrist is represented in the next descending part of the body of the bride, "the place that denotes the female". This part of the vision has generated much discussion among Hildegard scholars as well as interpreters of Catholic prophecy because of the location of the head of the Antichrist and the shocking nature of the illumination and its graphic description. But Hildegard explains the position of the monstrous head in strictly chronological terms. It directly corresponds to the harp in the Christ figure which is located in the "place that denotes the male". The location of the harp represents the time of the martyrdom of the faithful by the Antichrist; the harp itself represents,

> *"...the joyful songs of those who will suffer dire torments in the persecution that the son of iniquity will inflict upon the chosen, torturing their bodies so much that they are released from them and pass over into rest"*
> (Chapt. 9).

The two images, the harp and the monstrous head, reflect events that are happening concurrently. The shocking nature of the scene involving the Bride reflects the extreme violence of the persecution. The wounds in the upper part of the bride are from the forerunners of the Antichrist, the five beasts. The wounds and blood below the waist are from the more violent persecutions by the Antichrist himself.

The Sin of Greed

The importance of knowing that greed is behind the era dominated by civil unrest is that it reveals that the motive

64

behind the social uprisings is some level of economic disparity. While at present the list of millionaires and billionaires keeps growing, the middle classes and poor continue to see their standard of living decline. This could easily lead to social uprisings in parts of Europe and America. The 2005 Paris riots and the 2011 London riots, both reportedly motivated by economic hardship, may have been early warnings for what is to come; and by the numbers, the disparity today is much worse.

One is also reminded of the "Arab Spring" in 2011. Many if not all those uprisings, from Libya to Egypt to Syria was a revolution against to what were viewed as wealthy but corrupt leaders disinterested in the financial struggles of the people they govern, and who accrue fortunes at their expense. Also, in every one of those countries, once the status quo had broken down, Muslims turned on the small Christian populations with extreme violence, often with police refusing to intervene.

It is possible that these kind of clashes at some point and in some way could spill over to Europe due to its rapidly growing Muslim population and its declining Christian one. If current courses continue it is not difficult to entertain the possibility of a confrontation between the two. In Europe, unlike the nations that participated in the "Arab Spring", Muslims who are persecuting Christians would be joined in the effort by numerous radicalized groups that hate the Church and all it represents: anarchists, atheists, radical feminists, etc.

The "Fullness of the Gentiles" and "Great Apostasy"

It is especially important to take note that Hildegard tells us that by the time of the Grey Wolf the Church will have reached its' "full number of children." This is clearly a reference to something that the Bible plainly states must take place before the arrival of the end times: "...and this gospel of the kingdom will be preached throughout the world as a witness to all nations, and then the end will come" (Matt. 24:14). The Church's mission will have been completed. Hildegard does not associate this with a part of the bride's body, so we cannot know exactly when it will be accomplished. But it is reflected in the building which encompasses the figure of Christ, representing the completion of the Church for which Christ is the cornerstone.

One other event that the Bible declares must occur before the coming of the Antichrist is the great apostasy, a falling away of many Christians from the faith (Matt. 24:10-12; 2 Thess. 2:3). This event, however, is not directly addressed in Hildegard's vision. We can assume that she was aware of this, her extensive knowledge of the Bible as well as specific Church teachings on the end times is unquestionable. Consequently, one would expect some reference to an apostasy.

There are two possible allusions to a mass apostasy in these texts. The first is to take the first four eras together as this general apostasy, or great "falling away". In this regard it must be admitted that the Church has lost over this period, particularly in Europe, priests, nuns, religious brothers, etc. on a massive scale. And the statistics on the number of Catholics who routinely ignore Catholic moral teachings that they consider personally inconvenient are astonishing. Yet there is a problem with that view; the Catholic Church keeps growing. One would expect that during the great apostasy to see a major reduction in the number of professing Catholics. The Vatican keeps careful records on the annual change in the Catholic population throughout the world; and it has not been shrinking but growing, and there are presently about one billion members of the Church. An increase in the world's population might explain it, but it is difficult to refer to a numerically growing Church as experiencing a general apostasy.

A second possibility emerges when one considers that while there may be one billion Catholics worldwide, many of those counted are "nominal" Catholics, Christians in name only. Recent surveys reveal that while over eighty percent of Italians identify themselves as Catholic, only fifteen percent attend mass regularly, the number is less in France.[2] Yet is it not true that attending mass regularly is one of the minimal requirements for identifying someone as a true Catholic? What might be their fate when the Church will be "harshly reproached for her many sins".

Should some liability or physical danger be attached to identifying oneself and one's family as Christian, whether it may be in the form of social pressures, legal threats, terrorism, etc., it can be guessed that nominal Catholics would walk away, as well as many practicing Catholics. Adding up the number of non-practicing Catholics who identify themselves as Catholics in all of Europe leads to well over a hundred million people. The ones that come through this era will be the generation that resist the Antichrist and endure his persecution. It is doubtful that nominal Catholics and lukewarm Christians in general would be among them.

Summary

After the era of the Black Pig ends and the era of the Grey Wolf commences, there will be evidence of a spiritual renewal in the Catholic Church. The time will also be marked by widespread social uprisings aimed at people and institutions that are viewed as unfairly wealthy and will also involve violence toward the Church. There are many possible scenarios as to how this unfolds, yet Hildegard gave us more than enough information to clearly recognize the era of the Grey Wolf when it arrives, and to prepare for it.

VI

The Antichrist

After Hildegard's characterization of the era of the Grey Wolf, but before her portrayal of the Antichrist, a special message is embedded in-between the two in which God, through the voice of Hildegard, issues a stern warning. The message is not addressed to people of the twelfth century, but to those living in the era of the Grey Wolf. And it is directed specifically to teachers, referring to them in the chapter title as the "learned". Elsewhere in *Scivias* Hildegard often identifies teachers with clergy. It is a demand for them to heed the words of *Scivias* regarding the Saint's description of the Antichrist:

> *"O fruitful and rewarding teachers! Redeem your souls and loudly proclaim these words, and do not disbelieve them; for if you spurn them you contemn not them but Me Who Am Truth. ...But from now on the predestined epoch is fast approaching, and you are hastening toward the time when the son of perdition will appear. Grow therefore in vigor and fortitude, My elect! Be on your guard, lest you fall into the snare of death; raise the victorious banner of these words, and rush upon the son of iniquity. For those who forerun and follow the son of perdition whom you call Antichrist are in the way of error; but as for you, follow the footsteps of Him Who taught you the way of truth"* (Bk. 3, Vis. 11, Chap. 19).

If the foregoing analysis in this book is correct, and we stand in the latter part of the era of the Black Pig, the warning can be regarded as a directive to the many instructors of the Catholic faith living today. This would clearly include Catholic priests and scholars, but likely also comprise Catholic authors, publishers, journalists, bloggers, etc., anyone who assumes the role of instructor of the Catholic faith. This eight-hundred-year-old message finally finds its audience in the present time!

Overall, Hildegard's description of the Antichrist is typical of orthodox Catholic teaching in her day. He is an individual person who will ascend to power through a series of tricks that are viewed by the public as supernatural. He will be given authority to rule the world. There will be a demand for Christians to apostatize, followed by tribulations, etc. However, Hildegard adds many more details of the life of the Antichrist, particularly his early days, fascinating new elements of future history that will help Christians recognize the son of perdition long before the persecutions begin; awareness of these new details are meant to help us avoid falling "...into the snare of death". As in the analysis of the era of the Grey Wolf, we will first summarize those details of the life of the Antichrist and follow up with an inquiry as to their significance and how they might be manifested in the world at that time.

Hildegard on the Antichrist

Hildegard starts with the mother of the Antichrist, of whom she states begins learning "the arts of the Devil" in her infancy. We are told that she grows up apart from her family, and in the care of "abominable people" living in the "vilest of waste places". As she matures her parents do not recognize her, nor even the people who raised her. At some point, perhaps in her mid-teens (we are not told what specific age), she will be visited by the Devil in the guise of an angel. She will depart from her community and seclude herself under the guidance of this angel from hell (chap. 25).

At some point after this the angel commands her to engage in intercourse with a succession of men at the same time, with all participants remaining anonymous. She is impregnated by one of the men, but she will never know which of the men it was. Hildegard tells us that at this point Satan "...will breathe on the embryo. and possess it with all his power". (At this point we are reminded by the Saint that this is all done with the permission of God). After the baby is born the mother will show the infant boy to the people around her, declaring to them that she does not know who the father is or how she got pregnant. At the same time, although she had been given to a life of debauchery, she begins to observe a chaste lifestyle. The reaction of people to this will be to give her and her baby respect and even consider her holy (Chap. 25).

Just like his mother, the boy will be "nurtured by the Devil's arts" from a young age and will grow up in seclusion. Hildegard explains that while the boy is still a youth his mother, with the help of her "magic arts", will present her son to the broader public. We are not told his exact age, but Hildegard declares that it is before the age of maturity. His reception is positive; he is admired by both Christians and non-Christians and even "loved" by them. When he reaches the age of maturity, he will begin preaching a doctrine that is "clearly perverse" (Chap. 26). This inaugurates his gradual rise to international fame and power.

The strategy he uses to achieve his goal of world domination is to align himself with "...kings, dukes, princes, and the rich" (Chap. 27). To accomplish this, he employs his knowledge of the "Devil's arts", to deceive people into supporting him. He performs a series of miraculous events that appear supernatural, but in reality are only apparently so. Much of this, we are told, will center on an illusive ability to manipulate the climate. The Antichrist will "...bring forth fire and lightnings from heaven and raise thunders and hailstorms." All of these, she explains, will only be "illusions" (Chap. 27).

He will seem to cause people to get ill and then miraculously heal them. He will even raise the dead. Hildegard explains how he can accomplish this. A corpse, whose soul is in the hands of the Devil, will move as if alive, but remain dead. We are reminded again by Hildegard that this will be permitted by God, but she adds that it will only be allowed to occur a few times. He will also appear to cast out demons (Chap. 27).

At this point there will be two types of response to the Antichrist by the public: those who fully believe in him and follow him, and those who admire and believe in him, but also want to retain and continue practicing their Christian faith. The latter group will suddenly fall ill by the hand of the Antichrist. Doctors and medicines will be of no help to them, and the Antichrist will generously offer to miraculously cure them. Many accept his offer of healing and once cured, they are moved to abandon their faith and follow him exclusively (Chap. 27).

Hildegard explains the reason why God is permitting these deceptive miracles, which is the basis for why the Antichrist accumulates so many followers. It is to show those who remain faithful to God that Satan has no power over them. He can dominate only those who follow him and incite them to commit evil deeds (Chap. 30). The Saint then tells us what the nature of his "perverse" message is:

"And he will acquire for himself many peoples, telling them to do their own will and not restrain themselves by vigils and fasting; he will tell them that they need only love their God, Whom he will pretend to be" (Chap. 30).

She adds that he will encourage sexual immorality and people will feel fortunate to be living at this time, regarding earlier generations of Christians as fools for their formality, religiosity, and ignorance of God's love.

At this point he will prohibit baptism and the sacraments and will "throw out" the gospel of Christ. This is when his greatest deception occurs: he will arrange to be run through by a sword and die; he will be covered by a shroud, and then falsely rise from the dead. This will amaze his followers and his power will increase. He will produce a document that he claims will be for the salvation of souls, but in reality, Hildegard tells us, it is a "dire curse" (Chap. 31). The rest of the vision is a summation of the persecutions that will occur and the role of the two witnesses, Enoch and Elijah. The only novel detail we find in this part of the passage is that the Antichrist will be killed by being struck by a bolt of lightning after ascending to the top of a mountain.

Commentary

It is clear that Hildegard's vision of the Antichrist supplements the biblical evidence and is meant to provide the generation of Catholic Christians living at the time an ability to recognize him early and avoid being deceived by his apparent miraculous abilities and the general appeal of his early religious teachings. The information above is sufficient in itself to facilitate this early recognition, though some theorizing on how this might be revealed in society could be a worthwhile effort.

Since the "Antichrist" is the opposite of Christ, it was always generally assumed that he would be conceived illegitimately, though this is not attested to in scripture. Hildegard not only confirms this, but she adds information on his mother's life. It was Satan in the guise of an angel, mocking the role of the angel Gabriel, that directed her to conceive in an act of fornication that would guarantee that no human father could ever claim him. The Devil would be the father once he breathed his spirit into the embryo.

Mocking the Blessed Virgin Mary, the mother will suddenly become chaste and begin presenting the fatherless baby to people and for this she is admired and considered holy.

It appears that she is able to convince them that she had no knowledge of how the baby was conceived, suggestive of a miraculous virgin birth. With no father making any claim, and on account of her previously secluded lifestyle, this may be a possibility. It should also be noted that the surname of the Antichrist will likely be a matronymic, that is, he will have the same last name as the mother.

Her own experience growing up would be the model for his progress: seclusion from society, and a devotion to learning the " Devil's arts". This is doubtless a reference to the study of a selection of the many books written on occult practices that instruct in methods of commanding demons and casting spells. This is how the Antichrist will learn how to deceive people into believing he has miraculous power. On the other hand, he will command an ability to influence real-time events. In the classic eschatological work from the late nineteenth-century, *The End of the Present World and the Mysteries of the Future Life*, Fr. Charles Arminjon explains how the Antichrist will deceive people by his magic:

> It is well known that the devils, deprived of their original beauty and goodness, have not lost any of their powers. They can act on the elements, condense clouds and vapors, project lightning and unleash storms. As for miracles properly so called, God alone can perform them. A miracle is a derogation of the laws of nature which surpasses every creative force, whether human or angelic. Thus, the Antichrist will not work true miracles, but only false and apparent ones.[1]

Importantly, the Antichrist will to some degree be a public figure while in his youth, probably in his late teens, it is difficult to know exactly what Hildegard meant by "before the age of maturity". Elsewhere, she refers to the age of maturity as the age when marriage is permissible, for a male, about sixteen. The Antichrist will draw people to himself with a message that appeals to those who are both Christians and non-Christians. Hildegard calls them "the worshippers and the non-worshippers of God". The appeal of the youth will have been influenced by the mother's use of the occult, the "Devil's arts". This suggests that the youth will perhaps display an unusual skill with words or languages, or an exceptional superior intelligence, etc.

These events should be easy to recognize since the words of the young man will have a positive appeal to both believers and non-believers. They will be unified in their acceptance of his message. This unity might be significant in a broader social context; he might be praised for uniting what had been to some degree antagonistic parties. This message, however, according to Hildegard, will change when he is an adult; he will begin proclaiming a doctrine that she refers to as "clearly perverse".

In a later work by Hildegard, *Liber Divinorum Operum*, "Book of Divine Works", she receives another vision of the time of the Antichrist and offers additional details on the nature of his "perverse" message:

> He will teach that incest and similar vices are no sins. He will also maintain that there is no sin when flesh warms itself on flesh, just as we humans quite naturally are comforted by the warmth of a fire. He will explain to us that all the precepts of chastity are without any scientific basis.[2]

She continues with a direct quote from the Antichrist:

> And he will further tell believers, "Your moral principle of chastity has been established contrary to the natural law. Why should a man not be warm when we consider that there is a fire in his breath that causes his whole body to burn? Is it possible for him to remain cold when this would be contrary to his whole nature? And why should

human beings be forbidden to warm their flesh on the flesh of others? The one you call your 'Teacher' gave you a principal that goes beyond your natural capacity when he taught you to look at natural things in this way. But I tell you: you live only once in this dual situation as a cold pole and as a warm pole. Therefore warm yourselves without any qualms and have no doubt that this individual has given you instructions that are unreasonable."[3]

Such a lecture directed at the Catholic Church about sexual morality would not be uncommon in today's secularized society. What is different here is that the speech includes a direct attack on Christ Himself, and chastity in particular. It is also clear that the target of his attack includes the celibacy of priests.

The Antichrist will begin his road to world domination by forming strategic alliances with influential leaders, including the rich. Hildegard does not mention the ten kings that cede him their authority, nor the false prophet that precedes the Antichrist, who mocks the role of John the Baptist. But her reference to the leaders, whom she calls, "...kings, dukes, princes, and the rich", may or correspond with the ten kings. Similarly, the mother of the Antichrist appears to be a likely candidate for the false prophet, as she presents him to the public and teaches him the "Devil's arts".

Summary

Through Hildegard, God gives our generation and the ones to follow additional details on recognizing the "evil of evils" before his comes to power. While he uses trickery and illusions to advance himself, demonic powers are nevertheless at his disposal. These will be used from the outset in his campaign of self-promotion and his early messages will be appealing to Christians. His mother will be by his side throughout and there will be no one claiming to have fathered him.

With regard to the later message of the Antichrist which is specifically directed at Christians in which he promotes sexual immorality, we took note of the fact that it was not unlike lectures that we hear from many of today's leaders. The difference is the era of the Grey Wolf. Recall that the rope from the mouth of the wolf to the mountain was both black and white, symbolizing the people of the era. The white represented those who were "purified". The Church will have experienced a spiritual renewal by the time the Antichrist begins his rise to world domination. These will recognize him early and prepare themselves for what is forthcoming.

Conclusion

Each of the first four beasts attacked Western society and the Church in different ways, the pure blackness of the first four ropes connecting the beast to the mountain was meant to tell us that they would succeed. The history of the Church in Europe since the 1870s is unquestionably one of decline, a fall in mass attendance, vocations, spirituality, etc. The late nineteenth-century began a steady dechristianization of Europe and the West that has accelerated since the 1960s.

The identification of the first four beasts and their corresponding historical periods establishes a powerful case for the assertion that Hildegard's prophetic vision of the five beasts has been unfolding up to the present day. What makes the case so strong is that the eras follow the correct sequence and are not interchangeable. The wild and licentious era of the Pale Horse cannot correctly describe the main themes of the other three periods, nor could the war-mongering era of the Yellow Lion be associated with the other three which were relatively peaceful.

Certainly, licentiousness describes an aspect of the present era, but it will not likely be the historical legacy of Western society today in the same way as it was for the previous era in which a sexual revolution took place. The extreme and perverted nature of social engineering and its increasingly totalitarian drift are more likely to define the present period. Could four similar periods occur at some point in the future? The answer, of course, is yes. In an age of nuclear weapons WWIII would undoubtedly be more destructive than WWII; and another era of social injustice could lay ahead of us. Yet would it be reasonable to assume the possibility that five brief historical periods will appear sometime in the future that would have the correct attributes and follow the precise sequence as described by Hildegard? This seems improbable.

Nevertheless, a final judgment on the fulfillment of Hildegard's prophetic vision must be considered pending until the establishment of the era of the Grey Wolf, and it becomes evident that the events of that era correspond to her explanation of its symbolism. As the length of the rope indicates that the specific characteristics of the era will be perceptible from its beginning to its end, it will be apparent early on that Hildegard's prophetic vision of the five beasts has been unfolding before our eyes. At that point, the case should be settled and the faithful should prepare, physically and spiritually, to undergo testing.

In the meantime, an unknown number of years remain before the era of the Black Pig concludes. One should expect more laws that contradict natural law, ones that might be increasingly hostile in their attempt to force Christians to act in ways that are contrary to their faith. Again, the rope from the pig's mouth to the mountain was all black, symbolizing that this era also would be another losing battle for the Church. Hildegard's vision of this era does not include a broad spiritual revival until the following era.

Hildegard's Later Works

St. Hildegard had commented on the vision of the five beasts later in her life. In this study we elected not to incorporate that commentary in our effort to understand the vision's meaning. The reason is that there are inconsistencies between her descriptions of the symbolism in those later texts and the ones in *Scivias*. There are a number of academic studies of Hildegard's prophetic writings that argue that her conception of the last days had changed over time. They compare what is referred to as her early and later prophetic thought. For example, at one point she declared that the epoch of the Fiery Dog had commenced in her time. This is generally explained as her response to a deteriorating relationship between the Church and the Holy Roman Empire which had besieged the Papal States determined to control the Papacy.

However, it is not conceivable that the last days would have begun back in the twelfth century. As demonstrated here, the era of the Fiery Dog would not begin for 700 more years. Like this study of the visions in *Scivias*, a careful approach to her later prophetic texts from a distinctly Catholic perspective might unveil less of a contrast between her earlier and later views on the end times.

There is one last observation that emerged from this interpretation of the five beasts that is worth noting. Hildegard's prophecies about the future are not conditional. Some, but not all, credible Catholic prophecies consist of warnings that include conditions which, if met, would prevent or limit a chastisement or similar event. This is typical of many of the Church-approved Marian apparitions. With Hildegard there are warnings but no conditions; what she declares will happen in the era of the Grey Wolf will not be avoided. This is not contradictory but reflects the providence of God, who knows the outcome of all things yet provides opportunities for man to repent and turn to Him for redemption.

St. Hildegard's recent rediscovery, eight hundred years after her death, and her subsequent elevation to a Doctor of the Church was surely not without divine influence. She was entrusted with gifts for the benefit of the Church during the twelfth century, but that same Church will possibly need her help more in the twenty-first century.

Appendix: The Five Beasts and Revelation 17

If this book's theories are compelling, then it would be incumbent on us to look for biblical references to that same future period of time, those decades leading up to the appearance of the Antichrist. This would allow us to possibly confirm Hildegard prophecies through side-by-side comparisons. What we would be looking for are not necessarily exact correlations since apocalyptic literature can vary widely in its allegorical descriptions of the same historical events. The primary goal would be to look for the presence of material inconsistencies. Hildegard, however, knew her Bible as did Volmar, so contradictions between scripture and *Scivias* are not to be expected.

One such reference is the well-known apocalyptic passage in the Book of Revelation which includes the description of the infamous "Whore of Babylon" and the "Beast with Seven Heads". Unfortunately, the book of Revelation is exceedingly difficult to interpret, and Revelation 17:1-14, which references the Whore and the Beast, is especially confounding. Unlike Hildegard's visions, the imagery in this passage is not accompanied by detailed interpretation. But since it is clearly referencing the period of time leading up to the Antichrist, comparing it with the parallel account in Hildegard's prophecy is obligatory. We will uncover clear differences, though they appear to be immaterial. The similarities, however, are striking.

Biblical Typology

A common method of interpreting Revelation among Catholic biblical scholars is typological. It involves the study of words, events, symbols, etc. that have a broader meaning than their immediate context. Numbers connected to events are the most common "types" found in the Bible; there were forty days of rain, forty years in the Sinai wilderness, forty days fasting in the desert etc. It tells us that these events are connected or in some way foreshadowed each other. When a passage in Revelation can be connected to an event or series of events which happened in the first century, up to the time of St. John writing, it is likely that they were meant to foreshadow events in the future. Catholic biblical scholar Peter Williamson, in his popular commentary on Revelation prefers the typological approach to interpreting the book's message, noting that certain events in the first century were recounted in order to foreshadow events in the last days:

> ...[U]nderstanding the book's first-century historical context is essential for interpreting it correctly. However, it is also clear that Revelation claims to depict the Church's trials leading up to the return of Christ. ...In John's view, the spiritual dynamics of the final trial are already present in the temptations and persecutions that confront the Church in his day. From our vantage point centuries later, we can see that the prophet John saw the end of history through the lens of the trial facing the first-century churches of Asia in the Roman Empire. Like other eschatological [end-time] biblical prophecies, those in Revelation seem not to distinguish the author's day from that of history's end.[1]

Utilizing this approach for interpreting Revelation 17, we have a clear biblical reference to a series of brief historical periods that are typologically linked to the first century and lead up to the time of the Antichrist. The relevant text can be divided into two parts:

Revelation 17:1-6 (New American Bible, Revised Ed.)

"Then one of the seven angels who were holding the seven bowls came and said to me, "Come here. I will show you the judgment on the great harlot who lives near the many waters. The kings of the earth have had intercourse with her, and the inhabitants of the earth became drunk on the wine of her harlotry." Then he carried me away in spirit to a deserted place where I saw a woman seated on a scarlet beast that was covered with blasphemous names, with seven heads and ten horns. The woman was wearing purple and scarlet and adorned with gold, precious stones, and pearls. She held in her hand a gold cup that was filled with the abominable and sordid deeds of her harlotry. On her forehead was written a name, which is a mystery, "Babylon the great, the mother of harlots and of the abominations of the earth I saw that the woman was drunk on the blood of the holy ones and on the blood of the witnesses to Jesus."

Revelation 17:7-14

"When I saw her I was greatly amazed. The angel said to me, "Why are you amazed? I will explain to you the mystery of the woman and of the beast that carries her, the beast with the seven heads and the ten horns. The beast that you saw existed once but now exists no longer. It will come up from the abyss and is headed for destruction. The inhabitants of the earth whose names have not been written in the book of life from the foundation of the world shall be amazed when they see the beast, because it existed once but exists no longer, and yet it will come again. Here is

85

a clue for one who has wisdom. The seven heads represent seven hills upon which the woman sits. They also represent seven kings: five have already fallen, one still lives, and the last has not yet come, and when he comes he must remain only a short while. The beast that existed once but exists no longer is an eighth king, but really belongs to the seven and is headed for destruction. The ten horns that you saw represent ten kings who have not yet been crowned; they will receive royal authority along with the beast for one hour. They are of one mind and will give their power and authority to the beast. They will fight with the Lamb, but the Lamb will conquer them, for he is Lord of lords and king of kings, and those with him are called, chosen, and faithful."

In the first passage the angel introduces John to specific apocalyptic images and characters. In the second, the angel explains who and what they represent. The explanation, however, is complex and contains what seem like riddles. While there is no clear consensus among Catholic interpreters concerning what these passages are referencing, it seems evident that the beast with the seven heads refers to the Antichrist, or at least the "eighth king" does. The latter is referred to as

> "The beast that existed once but exists no longer is an eighth king, but really belongs to the seven and is headed for destruction" (17:11).

This is the same beast that was introduced in Rev. 13:1-18 and will be destroyed by Christ ("the Lamb").

The reference to the seven kings representing the seven hills would clearly have been understood by St. John as Rome, since it was commonly known as the city on seven hills. A coin minted by Emperor Vespasian depicts the goddess Roma resting on seven hills just as the image of the harlot did. John would have made this connection immediately. Note how the angel is surprised by John's amazement, implying that the connection with Rome should have been obvious. So we have the rise of the Antichrist, who will deceive the nations in the last days and be destroyed by Christ, being presented in connection with the Roman Empire during St. John's day. From a typological viewpoint, the angel is describing the last days using the analogous history of early imperial Rome. The angel explains that each of the seven hills represents a king, connecting it to the seven-headed beast. John would have understood them to be seven Roman emperors.

The Seven Kings

There is no consensus among interpreters of the book of Revelation as to how exactly the seven hills and the seven heads are intended to refer to the Roman Empire, though most agree that they do. If John's understanding of the history of the Roman emperors was similar to that of Roman historian Suetonius, then the angel's explanation of the beast in terms of the Empire would have been especially confusing since there had been twelve, not seven. Suetonius' first emperor would have been Julius Caesar and he included in his book, *The Twelve Caesars*, the brief reigns of Galba, Otho, and Vitellius.[2] Starting with Julius would have meant that Otho was the Antichrist figure, but he only ruled for three months before committing suicide.

On the other hand, if John viewed Roman history like the much more respected chronicler of Rome, Cornelius Tacitus, then it would have made clearer sense. In his *Annals of Imperial Rome*, Tacitus begins with Julius but states clearly that he did not claim the title of emperor. Galba, Otho, and Vitellius he considered usurpers who seized the throne but only for a few months each in the year AD 69 until Vitellius was defeated by Vespasian. Tacitus was a senator during the reign of Domitian and would have known how the emperors were regarded by the Romans in terms of legitimacy.[3]

Following Tacitus, the kings would have been the seven Roman Emperors beginning with Augustus (27 BC-AD 14), five of which, the angel tells John, have "fallen", or died. Following Augustus, they would have included Emperors Tiberius (14-37), Gaius (Caligula) (37-41), Claudius (31-54), and Nero (54-68). The next one, the "one who still is", would have been Emperor Vespasian (69-79), who seized the throne during "the year of four emperors". The seventh, Titus (79-81), whose reign lasted only two years, is the one who is referenced by, "...when he comes he must remain only a short while", leaving Domitian, the one who exiled John to the penal island of Patmos, as the eighth king.

The angel further helps John understand the beast's connection to the empire by referring repeatedly to an eighth king but who is really one of the seven who dies and then comes back to life to rule a second time: "...it existed once but exists no longer, and yet it will come again." John would have understood this to be a reference to a much-believed popular myth in the first century that the hated Emperor Nero's suicide was unsuccessful or faked. After being declared an enemy of the people by the senate and apparently committing suicide by stabbing himself before few witnesses, it was believed that he survived. He then went into hiding in Parthia with the intention of returning and re-establishing himself on the throne. Historians of this period refer to this legend as "Nero Redivivus".

Emperor Nero

> "Count the numerical values of the letters in Nero's name, and in 'murdered his own mother': you will find their sum is the same."

This is a typical piece of Roman graffiti during Nero's reign as reported by Suetonius.[4] It refers to Greek numerology. In Hebrew numerology (gematria), however, we know that his name adds up to the number of the Antichrist, 666. He did indeed murder his mother, as well as kick his pregnant wife to death when she complained about him coming home late. He also may have invented homosexual marriage, as on two occasions he publicly married a male lover (Nero dressed as the bride). What is significant is that he was the first Roman Emperor to systematically persecute Christians, including the murder of John's brother disciples, Saints Peter and Paul. This makes Nero a "type" of the Antichrist.

Tacitus reports that Nero, who was widely suspected of instigating the burning of Rome in AD 64 and performing songs on his private stage while fire engulfed the city, needed a scapegoat. The emperor chose to blame those who were popularly referred to, according to Tacitus, as the "notoriously depraved Christians". Tacitus did not like Christians, who he claimed were followers of a "deadly superstition", and who engaged in "degraded and shameful practices", also claiming that "...the human race detested them." His personal lack of sympathy for their fate is striking:

> Their deaths were made farcical. Dressed in wild animals' skins, they were torn to pieces by dogs, or crucified, or made into torches to be ignited after dark as substitutes for daylight. ...Despite their guilt as Christians, and the ruthless punishment it deserved, the victims were pitied. For it was felt that they were being sacrificed to one man's brutality rather than to the national interest. [5]

The persecutions ended after Nero's death but resumed in the latter part of the reign of Domitian.

Emperor Domitian, The Eighth King

After the brief reign of Titus, identified by the angel to John as the seventh king, his brother Domitian took his place. Most of the information about his persecution of Christians comes from early Christian sources. Note the reference to Nero in this quote from Eusebius of Caesarea's History of the Church:

Many were the victims of Domitian's appalling cruelty. At Rome great numbers of men distinguished by birth and attainments were for no reason at all banished from the country and their prosperity confiscated. Finally, he showed himself the successor of Nero in enmity and hostility to God. He was, in fact, the second to organize persecution against us.[6]

Suetonius documents that in the later part of Domitian's reign his treasury had run short of money.[7] This was when the extreme persecution began; he even passed an automatic death sentence on anybody descended from the Davidic line. Tertullian, in his most famous work, *Apologeticus*, also compares Domitian to Nero:

Nero was the first who assailed with the imperial sword the Christian sect, making progress then especially at Rome. But we glory in having our condemnation hallowed by the hostility of such a wretch. For anyone who knows him, can understand that not except as being of singular excellence did anything bring on it Nero's condemnation. Domitian, too, a man of Nero's type in cruelty...[8]

Identifying Domitian with Nero was not uncommon among roman writers of the period, but it does not exactly fit with the words of the angel who seemed to identify the eighth king as the exact same person as one of the seven (Nero). But this is typical of the biblical typologies in Revelation; they lack exactitude. Professor Williamson, who we quoted earlier, stated that apocalyptic literature in the bible is "...the future addressed through parallels with the present."[9] But he adds that those parallels will not always be perfect. We know that the Antichrist will try and mock the death and resurrection of Christ through a deception, after which the Church will endure its final persecution. This is reflected in the Nero-like but more expanded persecutions of Domitian, the last and most brutal of the kings represented by the seven-headed beast. Yet it is reported by Eusebius that Domitian relented and stopped the persecutions; again, he was a "type", a foreshadowing of the Antichrist.[10]

The Five Beasts of St. Hildegard

It was revealed to St. John that the last days would resemble the first days of the Roman Empire, its first eight emperors, all of whom are part of the same apocalyptic beast that represents the person of the Antichrist. St. Hildegard's vision of five beasts appears to correspond to the first five heads of the seven-headed beast, the "...five who have fallen", in three ways.

First, they both represent five successive and unique (as well as brief) historical periods that precede the Antichrist and, in some way, prepare his way. Chroniclers of Rome report how the five emperors ruled in distinct ways. Secondly, both periods of rule (the five beasts and the five kings) were heavily influenced by evil and under the influence of the spirit of Antichrist. Thirdly, in the fifth period of each series (the reign of Nero and the era of the Grey Wolf) a period of physical persecution of Christians begins that would end, but then resume under a future ruler, but with more intensity.

Then there is some dissimilarity, and it is primarily in the numbers. In Revelation there is one beast with seven heads plus one, the last of which is the person of the Antichrist, versus Hildegard's five separate beasts that precede the Antichrist. A possible way to reconcile this difference is to regard Vespasian and his two sons Titus and Domitian as together forming a single reign. Vespasian had formally changed the laws regarding succession of the emperorship, thus guaranteeing that his sons would inherit the Empire. Historians refer to it as the Flavian Dynasty. Though the five preceding Emperors formed the Julio-Claudian dynasty, they could groom whomever they wished to succeed them. Under

Vespasian, the Roman laws of succession would apply.

This would match up with the five beasts as follows:

The Fiery-Red Dog = Augustus

The Yellow Lion = Tiberius

The Pale Horse = Caligula

The Black Pig = Claudius

The Grey Wolf = Nero

Rise of the Antichrist = reign of Flavians, culminating with Domitian

Hildegard does not present the rise of the Antichrist as an "era" with specific characteristics like the previous historical periods but the culmination of them, so the above correlation is possible. The reign of the Antichrist is also described as a family affair by Hildegard, with his mother as his instructor and promoter. The historians of the period report that the Flavian family ran the Empire, with little change in personnel after the deaths of Vespasian and Titus. Moreover, at the end of the reigns of the "five who have fallen", Domitian was in his early twenties, confident that he would one day become Emperor. The Antichrist will likely be alive during the era of the Grey Wolf.

It is also interesting to note that a clear majority of biblical scholars date the writing of the book of Revelation around the mid-90s. If this was the case, then the reference to the "five who have fallen" does not make sense, as John was writing during the reign of Domitian; Vespasian and Titus had also died. The angel, then, is purposefully placing the setting of the vision in the reign of Vespasian, twenty years prior, which would have been undoubtedly confusing to John. How might John have tried to make sense of this?

Some scholars explain this by suggesting that John experienced this vision twenty years prior and did not write it down until his imprisonment on the island of Patmos. Others claim that it was common in Jewish apocalyptic literature of the first century to intentionally place prophecies in the past to give them more authenticity. A better possibility is that the angel wanted John to understand that the "five who have fallen", representing the Julio-Claudio dynasty, are distinct from the Flavians that followed.

Summary

Biblical typology is not to be understood as an exact blueprint of the future but to only foreshadow forthcoming events, the differences with the two prophecies do not appear to be relevant. Just as past history can be organized and divided in different ways by different historians, those with the prophetic gift might report the same series of events in the future in different ways as well. Moreover, and this is an important distinction, Hildegard's visions are not typological. She does not see historical events that foreshadow future events, but using symbolic imagery which she carefully explains, she sees aspects the future exactly as they will happen.

While there is not a perfect correspondence between the period leading up to the Antichrist in both Revelation and St. Hildegard, there are no material inconsistencies. The first of the two periods of persecutions revealed by St. John as foreshadowed in the reign of Emperor Nero, is envisioned by St. Hildegard as beginning sometime during the era of the Grey Wolf. In my analysis of her vision, this era will soon be upon us.

Notes

Notes to the Introduction

1. Hildegard of Bingen. *Book of the Rewards of Life.* Translated by Bruce Hozeski. Oxford: Oxford University Press, 1997, p. vii.

2. Baird, Joseph L. *The Personal Correspondence of Hildegard of Bingen.* Oxford: Oxford University Press, 2006, p. 138-139.

Notes to Chapter 1

1. Hobsbawn, Eric J. *The Age of Empire*: 1875-1914. New York: Random House, 1987, p. 6.

2. Ibid.

3. Davies, Norman. *Europe: A History.* New York: HarperCollins, 1998, p. 829.

4. Hobsbawm, *Empire*, p. 85.

5. EWTN Global Catholic Network. Accessed September 30, 2013. http://www.ewtn.com/library/encyc/p9etsimu.htm.

6. Burleigh, Michael. *Earthly Powers: Clash of Religion and Politics in Europe, from the French Revolution to the Great War.* New York: Harper, 2006, p. 344.

7. Ibid.

8. Ibid., p. 311.

9. Ibid., p. 340.

10. The Catholic Encyclopedia, 1917. Catholic Online. Accessed November 20, 2013. htencyclopedia /view.php?id=6550.tp://www.catholic.org/

11. Grosshans, Hans. *The Search for Modern Europe.* Boston: Houghton Mifflin, 1970, p. 178.

12. The Holy See. Accessed December 21, 2013. http://www. vatican.va/holy_father/leo_xiii/encyclicals/documents/h f_l-xiii_enc_15051891_rerum-novarum_en.html.

13. Ibid.

14. Ibid.

15. Ibid.

16. The Holy See. Accessed December 21, 2013. http://www. vatican.va/holy_father/pius_xi/encyclicals/documents/h f_p-xi_enc_19031937_divini-redemptoris_en.html.

17. Ibid.

18. The Holy See. Accessed December 21, 2013. http://www. vatican.va/holy_father/leo_xiii/encyclicals/documents/h f_l-xiii_enc_28121878_quod-apostolici-muneris_en.html.

Notes to Chapter Two

1. Hobsbawm, Eric J. *The Age of Extremes: A History of the World, 1914-1991.* New York: Random House, 1996, p. 6, 21.

2. Burleigh, Michael. *Sacred Causes: The Clash of Religion and Politics, from the Great War to the War on Terror.* New York: Harpercollins, 2007, p. 340.

3. Glover, Jonathan. *Humanity: A Moral History of the Twentieth Century.* New Haven: Yale University Press, 1999, p. 355.

4. *Ibid.*, p. 336

5. Manzower, Mark, *Dark Continent: Europe's Twentieth Century*. New York: Random House, 2000, p. 54.

6. Ibid., p. 61.

7. Glover, p. 196.

8. Ibid., p. 195.

9. Burleigh, *Sacred Causes*, p. 195.

10. Glover, *Humanity*, p. 21.

11. Grosshans, Europe, p. 349.

12. Ibid, p. 352.

13. Johnson, Paul, What the temptations on the high mountain mean today, *The Spectator,* Feb. 25, 2009. Accessed June, 3 2012.
http://www.spectator.co.uk/columnists/3388016/and-another-thing-42/

14. Glover, *Humanity*, p. 361.

15. Ibid.

16. Orwell, Sonia and Ian Angus, eds. *Collected Essays, Journalism and Letters of George Orwell, Vol. 3*. New York: Harcourt, 1968. p. 99.

17. Glover, *Humanity*, p. 384.

18. Ibid, p. 405.

Notes to Chapter Three

1. Hobsbawm, *Age of Extremes*, pp. 320ff.

2. Hitchens, Peter. *The Abolition of Britain*. San Francisco: Encounter Books, 2000, p. 219.

3. Ibid., pp. 12-13.

4. Zeldin, Theodore. *The French*. London: Collins Harvill, 1988, p. 138.

5. The Holy See. Accessed May 24, 2013.
http://www.vatican. va/

holy_father/paul_vi/encyclicals/documents/hf_p-vi_enc_25071968_humanae-vitae_en.html.

6. The Holy See. Accessed July 1, 2014. http://www.vatican.va/holy_father/benedict_xvi/speeches/2010/december/documents/hf_ben-xvi_spe_20101220_curia-auguri_en.html

7. Berman, Ronald, editor. *Solzhenitsyn at Harvard: The Address, Twelve Early Responses, Six Later Reflections.* University Press of America, 1980, pp. 39ff.

8. Ibid.

9. Ibid.

Notes to Chapter Four

1. The Holy See. Accessed june 21, 2014. http://www.vatican.va/holy_father/john_paul_ii/encyclicals/documents/hf_jp-ii_enc_06081993_veritatis-splendor_en.html.

2. The Holy See. Accessed June 14, 2014. http://www.vatican.va/holy_father/john_paul_ii/letters/documents/hf_jp-ii_let_02021994_families_en.html.

3. The Holy See. Accessed June 14, 2014. http://www.vatican.va/holy_father/john_paul_ii/encyclicals/documents/hf_jp-ii_enc_25031995_evangelium-vitae_en.htm.

4. Ibid.

5. Hollender, Paul. "Political correctness is live and well on campus near you," *Washington Times,* December 28, 1993.

6. Bloom, Allen. *The Closing of the American Mind.* New York: Simon and Schuster, 1987.

7. Hitchens, Christopher. *Abolition,* p. 3.

8. Ibid.

9. Johnson, Paul, *Spectator.*

10. Ibid.

11. Ibid.

12. Annual Red Mass Homily. December 12, 2010. Priests for Life. Accessed January 15, 2014. http://www.priestsforlife .org/ library/document-print.aspx?ID=3038.

13. "Where's the shame? Scandals may no longer end political careers." McClatchyDC. July 11, 2013. Accessed January 12, 2014. http://www.mcclatchydc.com/2013/07/11/196452_ wheres-the-shame-scandals-may.html?rh=1

14. Doughty, Steve. "It's gay rights laws that are intolerant, says Cardinal." *UK Daily Mail*, March 29, 2007.

Notes to Chapter 5

1. Chodakiewicz, Marek Jan, and Radzilowski, John, eds. *Spanish Carlism and Polish Nationalism: The Borderlands of Europe in the 19th and 20th Centuries.* Charlottesville: Leopolis Press, 2001, p. 35.

2. White, Hilary. "Italy's Last Catholic Generation? Mass Attendance in Collapse Among Under-30s." Life Site News, August 8, 2010. Accessed October 12, 2013. https://www. lifesitenews.com /news/italys-last-catholic-generation-mass-attendance-in-collapse-among-under-30s.

Notes to Chapter 6

1. Arminjohn, Charles. *The End of the Present World and the Mysteries of the Future Life.* Translated by Susan Conroy and Peter McEnerny. Manchester: Sophia Institute Press, 2008, p. 70.

2. Matthew Fox, ed. *Hildegard of Bingen's Book of Divine Works: With Letters and Songs.* Santa Fe: Bear and Company, 1987, p. 254.

3. Ibid.

Notes to the Appendix

1. Williamson, Peter S. *Revelation.* Grand Rapids: Baker

Academic, 2015, p. 276.

2. Tranquillus, Gaius Suetonius. *The Twelve Caesars*. Translated by Robert Graves. Baltimore: Penguin Books, 1957.

3. Tacitus, Publius Cornelius. *The Annals of Imperial Rome*. Translated by Michael Grant. New York: Penguin Books, 1983.

4. Suetonius, p. 231-232.

5. Tacitus, p. 365-366.

6. Eusebius, *A History of the Church From Christ to Constantine*. Translated by G. A. Williamson. New York: Penguin Books, 1989, p. 54.

7. Suetonius, p. 303.

8. Tertullian, *Apologeticus*, in *Ante-Nicene Fathers*, vol. 3, ed by Philip Schaff. Christian Classics Ethereal Library, 2009. Accessed March 2, 2014. http://www.ccel.org/ccel/schaff/anf03.iv.iii.v.html.

9. Williamson, p. 277.

10. Eusebius, p. 55.

About the Author

Mr. Turner received a Bachelor of Arts in Biblical Studies at Bethel University in St. Paul, MN. He attended graduate studies at Bethel Theological Seminary and The University of Chicago's Oriental Institute. Recently retired, Mr. Turner maintains the blog www.thefivebeasts.wordpress.com, conducts research, and devotes as much time as possible to his many grandchildren.

Made in the USA
Middletown, DE
22 September 2024

61259927R00068